FROM
THE GARDEN LIBRARY
OF

_____

THE POTTED HERB

THE POTTED HERB

Written and Illustrated by
Abbie Zabar

Stewart, Tabori & Chang
New York

Copyright © 1988 Abbie Zabar

The author gratefully acknowledges *Gourmet* Magazine for permission to reprint the recipe for Garlic Rosemary Tuiles.

Published in 1988 by Stewart, Tabori & Chang, Inc.
740 Broadway, New York, New York 10003

Library of Congress Cataloging-in-Publication Data

Zabar, Abbie.
  The potted herb.

  Bibliography: p.
  1. Herb gardening.   2. Container gardening.
3. Plants, Potted.   4. Herbs—Utilization.   I. Title.
SB351.H5Z33   1988   635′.7   87-18167
ISBN 1-55670-018-0

Distributed by Workman Publishing
708 Broadway, New York, New York 10003

10 9 8 7 6 5 4 3 2 1

Composed in Berkeley Old Style Book and Goudy Handtooled by Trufont Typographers, Inc., Hicksville, New York.

Printed and bound by Toppan Printing Company Ltd., Tokyo, Japan.

To
all those who want
a little garden in their lives

ACKNOWLEDGMENTS

It is a pleasure and privilege for me to acknowledge my co-workers and friends for their multifaceted help and sensitive contributions to my book. A note of thanks to:

Allen Haskell, for his inspiring and beautiful gardening creations; Sal Gilbertie, for always generously sharing his down-to-earth explanations; Elisabeth Woodburn, for her encouragement and support of my idea, although she has probably seen every gardening book imaginable; Mary Merris, who first appreciated my writing efforts; and Alice Martell, for her enthusiasm and good judgments.

Andy Stewart, for initially understanding and appreciating my work; Roy Finamore, my editor, for his ever-thoughtful and pertinent critical assistance, his care, and his concern; and Diana Jones for perfectly realizing and making sense of a lot of pieces of scrap paper.

Rebecca Davidson, Dawn Mello, and Lily Royer for their friendship and advice; and Joyce Davis, whose invaluable assistance in the assembling of this project runs a close second to her rare friendship.

Plus an extra tin of tuna for Timothy, who much to both my delight and annoyance, always managed to stay on top of things.

CONTENTS

PREFACE

o feel the lure of green things growing . . . that's gardening, and I'd rather be weary from working a garden than at ease from anything else.

It's no wonder that all the world's religions say the garden is the place to be. After all, until they bit the apple, Eden was the perfect state of happiness. It was a place of extreme beauty and delight, and we've been going after it ever since. If life is a trip, then we began in Eden and hope to end up in paradise.

For those of us whose gardens are planted between our mind and a sunny window sill, imagine the beauty and pleasure of growing potted herbs as small green expressions of garden design, rather than mere houseplants. Useful and quietly beautiful, herbs are simple to cultivate yet full of creative potential. And, when grown as herbal topiaries, they are little masterworks destined to receive greater attention and more compliments than anything else you've ever nurtured.

I was at first self-conscious about my interest in gardening, having once been accused of not being a farmer's daughter. I will always be an amateur gardener, but the fact that I was not born on a farm has become a major asset. My writing and illustrative studies are based upon firsthand knowledge stemming from my own experiments at trying to do more than grow a mere pot of herbs. I have learned and developed all of this myself, just as I believe others might do with some inspiration from this book. For me, gardening is a combination of design and horticulture; it's where I hope to merge an artist's eye with a gardener's medium.

If the truth be known, anyone can raise a potted herb. It's how we grow it that makes for something wonderful, a piece of aesthetic gardening that is reminiscent of the delicate perfection of Eden.

It seems like all work to one of my neighbors, who doesn't know what it means to garden. But for those of us who do it, a garden is a work of magic. Gardening is both stimulating and soothing. It quickens your senses while quieting the world. Herb gardening in pots is a microcosm of these larger experiences. To create, nurture, and cultivate these designs is a patient, thoughtful process that is good for both you and your plants. If it happened any faster, I'm afraid you'd miss the real action.

Summer 1987
New York City

THE BONNEFONT HERB GARDEN AT THE CLOISTERS

HERBAL BEGINNINGS

e seem to think that herbs—perhaps because they are such undemanding, hardy little souls—have been around forever. In fact, they have. According to Genesis, everything except the grass and trees was herbs. Both useful and ornamental, humble herbs have through centuries and civilizations been the creative impulse for some of the most original forms of gardening. They are purposeful plants with heady aromas and subtle hues and do not depend upon flowers for their beauty. Herbs provide a quiet and exquisite poetry, even in the most contained situations. Indeed, potted herbs are practical and inspired solutions for today's gardening time and spaces.

How reassuring to know that, in our age of instant obsolescence, we can still grow the descendants of the very herbs that were cultivated more than 2,000 years ago at villas in Herculaneum—and smell the same wonderful aromas. We can have the past flowering in the present. Although plant material is harder to identify than other physical remains, the ancient use of herbs has been confirmed by many experts. Archeologists and botanists recognize plants by studying root cavities, soil excavations, and pollen in carbonized plant remains. Horticulturists and art historians learn from ancient stone reliefs, vase paintings, and decorative wall murals about the use of herbs in foods, festivals, and rituals. From literary sources beginning with Homer, classicists and linguists read about the power and presence of herbs in Greek myths and daily life. Yet the Western world came rather late to herb culture. The Chinese like to boast that their pharmacopoeia of around 3000 B.C., which was based on the healing qualities of herbs, is the oldest in the world.

After the Greek and Roman civilizations passed, walled monastery gardens became the center of herb-growing activity. Cultivating useful herbs was more than a pastime for the cloistered monks; it was a way of life and vital to their existence. Forbidden to eat meat and committed to manual labor, growing herbs and studying these plants enabled the monks to help the poor and sick country people who lived outside the

monastery walls. Sources like *De Materia Medica*, by the Greek herbalist Dioscorides, described more than 500 plants and had come down through history as a standard reference work. At the time of the revival of learning it became the chief source of scientific pharmacy. Through it the monks learned to recognize which herbs could cure and which could kill, which could stop bleeding and which would cause bleeding.

For protection and seclusion, as well as for keeping out stray animals, early monastery gardens were enclosed by walls, clipped hedges, and fences. They had a straightforward, utilitarian layout: simple beds were planted in narrow strips or squares. This logical design prevented the herb gatherer from confusing the plants and dangerously administering the wrong medication. Ultimately, the orderly patterns of these monastic gardens would inspire and lead to the enchanting Elizabethan herb gardens, my own inspiration for container gardening.

As the gloom of the Dark Ages gave way to the radiant flowering of the late sixteenth and early seventeenth centuries, the desire to define the botanical and horticultural differences between herbs and flowers took precedence in gardening. There was a deep and glorious craving to understand the systematic beauty of nature, and the late medieval world

14

stressed the individuality of each plant. This led to the herbals, among the first printed books in Western civilization. They showed dissections of plants and attempted to draw fruits and flowers naturalistically, rather than decoratively.

This was a time not only for the blossoming of new ideas and great discoveries; it was an age of romance as well. Heady scents filled the air as men and women of the aristocracy—wearing elaborately embroidered costumes depicting their love of flowers—strolled within beautiful and enchanting settings. There were camomile paths between lavender borders and seats of thyme beneath topiaried walls of clipped rosemary. It was an age of precious and practical wisdom, when William Lawson could suggest in his popular little guide, *The Country House-wife's Garden* (1617), that we should all have plenty of time to sit in our gardens.

In 1584, in the first book on gardening printed in the English language, Thomas Hyll directed his readers to plant herbs in separate plots of equal size. Each bed was to be enclosed with stone curbing or boarding and no bold herb was permitted to stretch beyond this limit. To prevent this, the sides of the plot were to be sheared in a hedgelike fashion. Thus continual trimming would bring out fresh new leaves, and both the tidy gardener and the cook would be satisfied. Appearance would be rigid and neat and the young leaves best for flavor. "Threads of knots and mazes should be made with hyssop, thyme, lavender cotton, and other evergreen herbs which could be neatly clipped," wrote Hyll, and these very same herbs are still perfect, four centuries later, for potted herbal topiaries.

POTTED HERBS FLOURISH OUTSIDE IN THE SUMMER AND CREATE VISUAL FOCUS

CULTIVATING

P lant propagation is a miracle no matter what method you choose, and nothing is more thrilling than seeing the first signs that you have begun a new plant successfully. It's a satisfaction that is shared equally by the amateur and the professional grower.

Herbs can be started either from seeds or vegetatively—by layerings, divisions, or cuttings. Although individual herbs lend themselves better to one technique than to another, the quickest route to a mature plant is through vegetative propagation. If the idea of plant propagation seems intimidating, remember the time you put a broken-off little stem into a glass of water. Sure enough, some roots formed. Vegetative materials want to continue to grow, so if you are at all conscientious about culture, you will probably get the plant you wanted.

SEEDS

Starting herbs from seeds is certainly the longest route to a finished plant, but you will have germinated a new plant from the true beginning. You might even be surprised by the appearance of your second-generation plant, since hybrids each have their own dominant hereditary traits and not all of them come true from seed. This method also allows you to put to use seeds that you might have gathered on your own. I can't imagine a more treasured souvenir than successfully germinated seeds brought back from a weekend trip.

Seed propagation is preferred for nonwoody producing herbs such as basil, dill, and parsley. (These tend to be short-lived annuals.) Begin with viable seeds from a variety that really interests you, or gather them yourself from a favorite herb. Shake the plant or rub some seed pods off when they are mature. (William Lawson advises, "Gather all your seeds dead, ripe, and dry.") Set these seeds aside on a napkin or plate for a few days because they need a period of dormancy, "after-ripening," before planting.

Take a 2½-inch clay pot, and cover the hole at the bottom with some shards of broken clay pots. If you haven't been gardening long enough to have shards lying around, break a pot that isn't important to you. You can plant in a used pot; just make certain that you soak it in soapy water and ammonia. Then scrub it with steel wool to remove any undesirable deposits on the interior and around the lip.

Fill the container with a fine-textured potting mixture that has been thoroughly wetted the night before but is not soggy at the time of sowing. A good mix for starting herb seeds is two parts sterilized soil, two parts coarse sand (like children's play sand, not beach sand), two parts finely milled sphagnum moss (to make the mixture more porous and water-retentive), and one part perlite. And that's it. Herbs do not need or want an enriched growing medium. This combination of ingredients is an inexpensive and ideal blend that will support the seeds during germination and rooting, while fostering good drainage. It can be kept evenly moist, which is so vital in the early stages of any form of plant propagation. Nutrients can be added later.

Tamp down the mixture in the pot with the bottom of another small flowerpot. This will eliminate air pockets and ensure even germination. The soil should come to about ½ inch from the pot's rim. Lightly scatter a few seeds over the moist surface, being careful not to let them clump together. It might seem obvious, but

Sprinkle tiny seeds from a folded piece of paper.

you should never plant more than one seed variety in a container. Dust a thin layer of sand and sphagnum moss over the seeds after sowing. The heavier sand will help drainage and prevent the tiny seeds from floating around, yet will be fine enough to drain quickly. The sphagnum moss lessens the threat of damping-off, a fungus disease that attacks seedlings in the early stages of breaking ground.

Spray the top with a fine mist, being careful not to upset the good work you've just done. Place a glass plate, covered by a piece of opaque paper, over the pot to keep moisture in and light out. Try to keep the soil evenly damp but not soggy. Although the seeds can't be allowed to dry out, their newly forming roots should not be surrounded by a wet mess; roots also need oxygen in the soil to survive. It is a delicate balance that is crucial to the successful germination of seeds and the formation of seedlings.

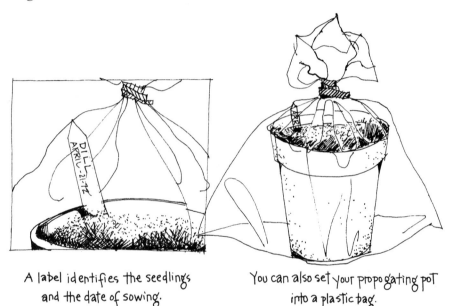

A label identifies the seedlings and the date of sowing.

You can also set your propogating pot into a plastic bag.

Move the whole set-up to a warm location whose temperature remains at about 70 degrees. Using a pencil or indelible pen, note the name of the seeds and the date of planting on a plant label and lay it across the top of the dish. It might be necessary to mist the soil surface again before the seeds start to break ground. Depending upon several conditions, this could take from a couple of days to a couple of weeks and in some unusual circumstances—like parsley, marjoram, bay, and sweet woodruff—even longer. When the seeds have sprouted and you've finished admiring your achievement, remove the covers and place the pot in good but indirect light. This will allow the roots to firm up without draining the plant's system from intense sunlight.

The first set of leaves that will appear when a seedling germinates are the *cotyledons*, or seed leaves. These are quite different from the characteristic adult leaves. After the seedlings have developed one set of true leaves, transplant each seedling to its own pot. Fill a couple of 2½-inch pots with your potting-soil mixture. Water, tamp down, and punch a hole in the soil with a chopstick or pencil. While holding the seedling by its true leaves (not the stem), delicately lift it up and out of the propagation pot. Replant the seedling in its new pot with the roots dangling straight down. Bury the stem up to the lowest leaves and, if anything, a tiny bit lower than it was previously planted in order to stimulate side-root formation. Gently move and press the soil in and around the stem. Mist water from above, and remember to keep the new transplant evenly wet. Water cautiously until new growth begins. This can be done from below by setting the clay pot in a basin of water up to its rim; when the surface is wet, the job is complete.

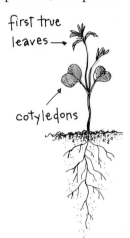

first true leaves →

cotyledons

Push the identification label into the soil mix, and place the plant in a sunny location to encourage sturdy seedlings that will not grow long and spindly. Most herbs need lots of light, and a window that receives several hours of sun a day will make your potted herb garden flourish. Your herbs will subsist in less light, but they will thrive in more. Rotate the pot so that the plant will not grow lopsided.

To encourage abundant foliage growth, fertilize with a dilute solution of fish emulsion about two weeks after transplanting. If you are blessed with more seedlings than you expected, give them to appreciative friends.

ROOT DIVISIONS

Root divisions are easy methods of vegetative propagation for low-growing herbs like chives, mint, thyme, marjoram, tarragon, and oregano. This method creates new plants with little expense, no fancy equipment, and minor effort. It is also almost foolproof, since you are already using part of a plant with its root system intact. Division is used mainly for rejuvenating the original herb or for propagating multiples of the parent plant; it is seldom worthwhile on young herbs or ones that are more than 2 feet tall.

Root divisions are best made in early spring. (This is the time when the plants have come to life and are active again.) Select a full perennial herb and pull it apart by its roots with your hands, or cut the root mass into a couple of sections with a sharp knife. Fill clean 5-inch pots with a moist mixture that contains 2 additional tablespoons of premoistened peat to encourage quick root healing and development. (As the peat moss takes a long time to absorb moisture once it is in the soil, it can create dangerous pockets of dryness if it is not prewetted.) Then plant each division separately.

Keep the plant out of direct sunlight for a couple of weeks until its system has recovered from the shock of division. You can fertilize with a light solution of fish emulsion only after the plant starts to produce new green growth.

A strong plant can yield one root cutting or several

cut line

LAYERING

Many plants naturally layer themselves when their low-lying branches rest along the ground. Layering is an easy and certain method of propagation because the new plant-to-be is nourished from the mother plant while its own root system develops. For this reason it is used to make cuttings from herbs that might otherwise not root easily and is a simple way of propagating sage, thyme, lavender, santolina, perennial marjoram, and other herbs that produce numerous low, flexible branches.

Use a soil mixture that has been lightened by adding 2 additional tablespoons of sand or moistened peat moss so that the medium will hold water yet drain easily. Bend a supple low-lying branch from the parent plant onto the soil of the new pot. With a clean knife make a slight cut or scratch in the bark near a joint in the branch. This will expose tissues with root-forming potential and hasten the layering process. For additional insurance you can dust the wound with a root-inducing hormone powder. Remove the lower leaves from the branch, and anchor it down firmly with a large hairpin, a bent nail, or a heavy stone. Cover the pegged-down portion with some soil mixture. Keep the whole set-up moist but not soggy.

In a few weeks lift out the peg; if the branch stays put it has probably rooted. Separate the new plant from the parent stock by cutting them apart carefully below the soil line. Since the new plant is already growing in its own container, no further transplanting is needed for some time.

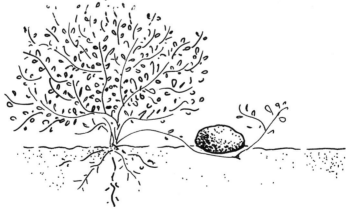

Hold down a bent low-lying shoot with a heavy stone.

FERTILIZING

In addition to being more aromatic and flavorful, herbs become stronger plants when they are grown in poor soil that is often reminiscent of their natural habitat. Atmospheric conditions such as light, temperature, and humidity, rather than fertilizing agents, contribute to the concentration of the essential oils that make an herb an herb.

Nevertheless, one important reason for growing potted herbs is to produce plants with lush foliage that can be pruned and shaped. Toward this goal, potted herbs should be fed with an organic fertilizer that is high in nitrogen; this will promote good green shoots and leaf growth. All herbs respond best to natural fertilizers like animal manures for outdoor herb gardens and fish emulsions for potted herb gardens. These are slow-acting fertilizers that encourage, rather than inhibit, the build-up of essential oils.

Fish emulsion is made of saltwater fish, and it does not burn when used as directed. It is a thickish liquid that is commercially packaged by several companies, and it can be readily bought at garden centers or neighborhood houseware stores that sell plant supplies. Dilute solutions can be applied twice monthly during periods of active growth. At the beginning of the growing season, you can also scratch some Electra—a powdery, slow-release organic fertilizer—into the potted soil mixtures or use it as a top dressing for long-term nourishment.

Never feed an herb plant—or any other plant, for that matter—that is resting, cut back, or not growing actively. Other than that, don't worry too much. Just be careful not to overfeed.

THOSE CREEPY CRAWLERS

I'm not bragging, but my herbs are never really bothered by critters. Yet that isn't to say it can't happen. Except for the bees and butterflies that love hovering around lavender and thyme flowers—and I love having them hover—most bugs have no interest in herbs. Chewing insects prefer to dine on less strong-smelling and milder-tasting leaves. In fact, herbs are very often used as companion plants in vegetable and flower gardens precisely because they help keep bugs away. Organic gardeners plant white-flowered scented-leaf geraniums amongst their vegetables because the blossoms are poisonous to the troublesome Japanese beetles, which are attracted to the flowers' scent and form.

Like most of us, I do not enjoy bugs, nor do I like to use pesticides or unsafe methods to control insects. Instead, I try to practice non-chemical prevention, especially on edible herbs. It's the simplest and safest cure.

This is my convenient and effective routine for clean and healthy herb plants that are grown in pots. Regularly wash the herbs either by sponging them down, spraying them down, or turning them upside down in a sink filled with liquid soap that has been diluted in lukewarm water. Of course, if you apply the soap solution forcefully with strong pressure from a hand-pump sprayer, you can dislodge the insects even more efficiently. I'd recommend that you use any mild liquid soap that you have in the house that you would use on your hands. It's convenient and nontoxic to you and your environment. Rinse the plant with clear water to remove residual soap layers that might cause leaf burn. Although these soap solutions do have emulsifying and spreading qualities, they do not continue to kill later-blooming insects.

Plan on doing this procedure once a month as routine plant hygiene. On a regular basis, especially during the drier winter months, this simple course will keep the herb foliage at its best. If you stay on top of things, this method is most useful when a short-term reduction of an insect population is necessary; a short-term infestation is probably the only kind that your potted herbs might have.

GOING OUTSIDE

If at all possible, try to give your potted herbs an outdoor place in the sun when the warm weather comes around. They'll resume their better natures and fortify themselves for the whole coming year, while adding charm and interest to any setting. Herbs in pots are one of the few houseplants that love to languish for hours in direct sun, but acclimate them to their vacation site slowly. Set them in a wind-free shady area for a week or two. Then you can move them to direct sunlight. Once outside they will need more water, more fertilizer, and more pruning. In return they will become more beautiful.

On my wide-open windy terrace gardens I surround a favorite bench with all of my potted herbs, and I stabilize the taller topiaried herbs against the wind with large and attractive stones. I do my watering in the first moments of the morning, when the city is magically still and the only sounds come from the very active bird life. It's the most peaceful and optimistic moment of my day, a time when anything and everything still seem possible.

When the daylight hours start to shorten you should think about bringing your plants back inside. Stop weekly fertilizing around the middle of August so that the herbs will not be puffed up with nitrogen-lush growth. Wash the leaves and the pots with some soapy water and a good spray of the hose; then prune them into tight shapes.

Like any well-mannered guest, potted herbs shouldn't overextend their visit. It is more important for them to get comfortably reacclimated indoors than to catch the last rays of summer sun—or, worse yet, the first frost of fall. If the light source is too abruptly reduced, it will be impossible for a plant to support all of its full new growth.

25

COMELY CLAY POTS

In truth, you can grow an herb in anything. I have seen them growing everywhere and out of everything. A precious little wild herb sprouts between rocky crevices in its natural Mediterranean habitat, seemingly undernourished, sun-baked, windswept, and sprayed with salt air. Yet it looks more beautiful and grows finer than anything you could ever imagine. Herbs will live in old English terra-cotta chimney pots or half-round beer kegs formed from oak staves. Antique sinks or stone troughs that might have once collected rain water from under the eaves of farm buildings can hold a planting of herbs, nestled as if in a rock garden.

As long as you provide drainage holes or a layer of pebbles at the bottom of a container, your choices might seem limitless. Understand, however, that containers are made from different materials for different purposes. There are nonporous plastic pots, which are very good at retaining moisture in hot greenhouses. Peat pots and peat pellets are transitional containers, with thin walls made of compressed peat that allow the plant's roots to penetrate the moist sides. They can be transplanted directly into the garden—seedling, peat pot, and all—without disturbing the new root system. Then there are glazed clay pots that are made from terra cotta but have been fired with a finish, either for appearance or to inhibit the natural porosity of the material. The nearest that I came to using glazed terra cotta was occasionally applying a couple of coats of clear nail enamel to the underside of a clay pot because I wanted to sit it on a surface without a saucer and without leaving a watermark.

The choice of a container is a personal one, but you should never underestimate the importance of the right pot. Different materials may come and go, yet for my gardening there is nothing better than the old-fashioned unglazed clay pot. It is classically beautiful and functionally correct. The porosity discourages soil from stagnating, while the fade-away appearance has just the right amount of presence. Best of all, herbs seem to bask in the natural beauty of clay.

The appeal of Andalusian pot culture is not lost on me. In this region of southern Spain, bordering on the Atlantic and Mediterranean, charming examples of traditional folk gardening appear in unstudied design elements. Along the streets, humble structures have stuccoed walls totally covered by simple plants in clay pots.

Many people suffer from "terraphobia"—the fear of exposed clay pots—but for me the second-best sight in a greenhouse has always been the half-height walls of assorted terra-cotta shapes. The older, more distinguished examples proudly display their well-earned beauty marks. They have a stained patina about them that, happily, no amount of soaking will erase. Their rims are more often than not punctuated with chips and scratches. Over time their bright coloring has mellowed and lost any original luster it might have once reflected. These pots are no longer factory-slick but visual reminders of the land itself. After all, "terra cotta" means "baked earth."

I constantly gather clay pots from other places and other times—from a New England town like New Bedford or from the remote provincial French village of Biot; I tend to associate locations with their terra-cotta spoils. It is no wonder that whenever and wherever I travel, I feel weighted down by strangely shaped underseat parcels marked "TOO FRAGILE." Flowerpots, as they are most often called, can of course be found in all the obvious locations, like plant stores, garden centers, nurseries, and even the local Woolworth's. But if you want something special for your prized cultivar, you should start looking in less familiar places. I have found the disparate pieces of my own private collection of clay pots and planters at abandoned greenhouses, specialty growers, foreign nurseries, unassuming yard sales, and presuming antique shops. Your mind must be open and your eyes curious to recognize the potential of early terra-cotta ware. Just know that if you see what you like and if you can afford it, buy it now. After all, as with most cherished things in life, we tend to remember clearly those things we never got.

I made one of my best discoveries during the last moments of a winter vacation in Cap Ferrat. I finally decided to turn down the driveway that was marked with a tempting hand-lettered sign, "Horticulture." Every square centimeter along the steeply pitched road was lush with over-grown vegetation. In the distance I could see carefully landscaped trees and bushes, but somehow they had a "For Sale" quality about them. It seemed no one was around when I nearly tripped over a few casually discarded clay pots. They were pale, plain, and elegant, suggesting the rimless pots of ancient cultures. Like a boar sniffing for truffles, I followed their path. All of a sudden, in neat rows reminiscent of planting fields, there were ranks and files of these generic pots.

A perpetually suntanned workman dressed in his *bleu de travail* appeared. In half-English, half-French, I told him that I liked the pots. He looked at me with a puzzled expression and pointed to the nursery plantings. With an urgency that overcame all language barriers I insisted that I was more interested in the pots. He shrugged his shoulders and threw me a to-each-his-own-pleasure look. Within minutes I had gathered a minor stockpile. I turned each pot over, testing for cracks by making them ring like bells, weighing their merits, judging for character. At last I culled down my prospective collection to thirty-eight and anx-iously asked what the price would be. Still somewhat confused by my enthusiasm for his common garden-variety pots, he couldn't come up with an answer, so I suggested an amount that quickly convinced him of my sincerity, and I added a few extra francs for the packing material. After all, the man took the precious straw mulch right out of his vegetable garden. The pots were quickly bundled and carefully laid into a brick-layer's canvas carry-on tote that I always travel with for just this kind of cargo. We smiled and shook hands, and I raced off to catch my plane back to New York.

I also treasure several early twentieth-century English pots of dark terra cotta brought back from other trips. With the interest in clay pots of different origins unwittingly comes a bit of awareness. I see how the earth, water, and firing conditions of the Mediterranean make for a more porous container, unlike the heavier and darker clay pots of northern Europe. It seems as fundamental as making bread. The indigenous water, flour (or earth), and firing method can make the same recipe taste and look different. A long crusty baguette with a dense white fill becomes lighter and airier in Greece, Spain, or even the south of France. Likewise for clay pots.

The English pots are very sturdy-looking, and, with true na-tionalistic pride, each one is neatly stamped "Made in England." The prize of the collection is an exceptionally heavy rectangular clay flat that was originally used for starting seeds. In my garden it now "runneth over" with a form-fitting mat of woolly thyme (*Thymus hirsutus*) that makes it look like a fluffy crate of greenery; in fact, it has become its own topiary shape. The English pots attempt to run true to some kind of sizing, but I like all of their quirky little variations. To me they are an expression of a

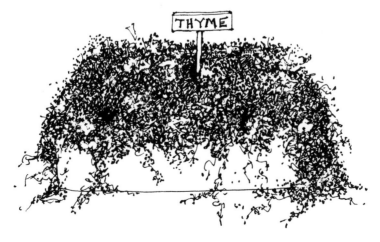

handmade craft that is soon to become an endangered species. I imagine that one day, after the whole world turns to plastic, humble clay pots will finally be valued and studied like objects made of more precious materials.

Here are two very interesting sources for beautiful contemporary clay pots and unique antique pieces:

Jim Keeling describes himself as a "specialist thrower of horticultural wares." He upholds the traditional methods of making magnificent large ornamental garden pots; along with these he offers an extraordinary selection of smaller hand-thrown varieties that are all formed from a mixture of local clays. They are guaranteed frostproof against laminating for ten years.

In 1985, as a testament to the beauty of terra cotta, Keeling was awarded a Winston Churchill Traveling Fellowship as a "flower potter," which allowed him to study in Italy and increased his design repertory to include ornately encrusted pots decorated with garlands and other classical motifs. He offers a free illustrated catalogue and will ship to the United States. Contact him at:

> Jim Keeling, Flowerpots
> Whichford Pottery
> Shipston-on-Stour
> Warwickshire, CV36 5PG
> ENGLAND

Since 1986 Sotheby's auction gallery has organized a "garden statuary and architectural items sale," held, appropriately, in the Sussex countryside during the last week of May and again at the end of September. Just about every type of garden decoration and accessory can be found here, whether the material be lead, cast iron, wrought iron, wood, bronze, marble, stone, composition, or terra cotta. A recent sale featured a graduated set of terra-cotta pots decorated with beribboned swags, a couple of carved stone garden urns with lions' heads, and several pairs of prized Gertrude Jekyll terra-cotta jardinières with scroll handles, any one of which would be perfect to show off a splendid topiary. But it is also possible to go antiquing without ever leaving home. You can order from a current catalogue. Contact:

Sotheby's
1334 York Avenue
New York, New York 10021

For catalogue and bidding information,
call (212) 628-4604 or (800) 752-5686.

It is fascinating to see how cultures repeat themselves, as contemporary terrace plantings evoke ancient Greek rituals of growing plants in containers on patios and rooftops. During the Festival of Adonis women planted quick-sprouting grass and fennel seeds in unglazed earthen pots; these were placed as offerings around statues of the youth on the roofs of houses. In the hot sun the plants quickly germinated and died just as rapidly, symbolic of the lovely, fresh, and brief life of the mythical hero. The festival signified the course of the seasons; it represented the spring after the winter.

An excavation in the 1930s unearthed a deep trench around the well-preserved Athenian temple known as Theseum, northwest of the Acropolis. Long rectangular pits, which surrounded the columned sanctuary, dedicated to the Greek hero Theseus, held the remains of broken clay flowerpots once used to propagate tree cuttings. The trench was dug to hold potted saplings, which would ultimately form a promenade where Greek statesmen could stroll under a shaded canopy of trees and discuss the events of the day.

In 160 B.C. the Roman writer Cato gave instructions on the use of terra-cotta pots. In his *De Re Rustica*, the oldest surviving literary prose work in Latin, he wrote in the plain style of a farmer's manual: "To make shoots take root while on the tree, make a hole in the bottom of a pot and push the branch that you wish to root through it. Fill the pot with earth, press it thoroughly, and leave it on the tree. When it is two years old, cut off the branch . . . shatter the pot and plant the branch in the pit together with the pot."

So much for modern-day peat pots and contemporary air-layering culture. It is horticulturally humbling to discover that we are still working with techniques, materials, and accessories that are centuries old. Indeed, clay pots have always been and always will be a beautiful and functional part of gardening.

LITTLE POTS OF STORE-BOUGHT HERBS ARE THE EASIEST WAY TO START YOUR GARDEN

SOME HERBS TO GROW

Herbs are easy to grow, easy to eat, and easy to like. And when grown in pots they will provide an herb garden all year long. Even when it's cold and rainy, you won't have to pull on a pair of Wellington boots to walk in your garden. They are valued for their flavorful, aromatic, medicinal, and sometimes mystical properties; it is almost easier to say what herbs are not. They are not trees, although they might be woody, nor are they food crops or spices. Herbs cover a wide range of botanical families, and an herb to one person might be a nuisance to someone else. Pennyroyal and spearmint are delicious for iced tea, but not if you want a perfect lawn.

An herb can be defined as a plant that dies back to the ground after flowering, implying that it has no hardwood structure like trees or shrubs. Yet some of the plants that I've selected for use in my potted herb gardens are valued precisely for their ability to become woody; we want twiggy species for herbal topiaries. Rather than being appreciated for their flowers, herbs form a delicate and soothing green vision with nature's best color. The palette ranges from the silvery artemisia, santolina, and lavender to the elegant evergreens of bay, myrtle, and germander. Some herbs, such as rosemary, even exhibit alternate shades of green on the underside of their leaves.

Here is a potpourri of herbs that are especially responsive to pot culture. When grown as herbal topiaries they will not only look better from year to year, but, like fine wines, their flavors and aromas will improve with age. Begin with this group. They'll grow on you.

A NOTE ON NOMENCLATURE

The good news is that botanists everywhere speak the same language. The bad news is that maybe Latin's not your native tongue. Yet the botanical name of a plant, which is usually Latin, is a universal tool and a lovely aid. It is a plant label that is understood by gardeners around the world. Many of us use it unknowingly already—geranium, chrysanthemum, fuchsia, rhododendron. . . .

The basis for the binomial system of identification for all organisms, including plants, was established by the Swedish botanist Linnaeus in the eighteenth century. This terminology is both instructive and interesting, and that is why I use the botanical name in italics, along with the more familiar or common name of the herb.

BASIL (*Ocimum* varieties)

There are fewer plants with more contradictory associations than basil. It was considered the sacred plant of India, and it was cultivated around every temple as a form of divine protection; in addition, the Hindus filled the interiors of these hallowed structures with pots of *tulasi*, the sacred perennial basil. But Western cultures endowed the herb with both good and evil qualities. Whereas the Greeks put curses on the strongly aromatic leaves, to most Romans, basil's perfume was thought to cause sympathy between two people and was a sign of love. It was said that a man who accepted a sprig of basil from a woman would love her forever, while a pot of basil on the balcony showed that a lady was welcoming her suitor's advances. In spite of its diverse interpretations, basil proved to be a valuable herb and was actively traded throughout the world, from India to Asia Minor, from Greece to Rome, and from northern Europe to America. Sweet basil is one of the herbs mentioned in our colonial garden records.

Basil is an annual herb that is related to mint. It has a pungent, clovelike aroma, and its botanical name is derived from the Greek verb meaning "to be fragrant." Whether we are growing sweet basil (*O. basilicum*), bush basil (*O.b. minimum*), lettuce-leaf (*O.b. crispum*), or dark opal basil (*O.b. purpurascens*), all of our basils have similar cultural requirements. Set the seed in early spring, barely covering it with your soil mixture, and germination should occur in less than a week. Basil is highly sensitive to cold, so put the pots outside only when the danger of frost has absolutely passed. Place them in a sunny but sheltered spot, and water them well during the summer's midday heat. Take your first cutting across the main stem, leaving at least one node with two young shoots intact. The remaining growth will branch out and be ready for trimming in another two to three weeks, while starting to form a bushy little plant. Feed the herbs regularly after each harvest to encourage new leaf production.

Rather than flowering all at once, basil produces a succession of white blossoms that start at the lower part of the stem. Although these flowers are lovely to look at and are a favorite of bees, the plants will grow best if pruned before they bloom. By continually cutting them back, the dwarf varieties will grow into small, puffy bushes. Pots of them set in format will make unusual and attractive annual borders around flower and vegetable gardens.

Since ancient times basil was one of the few flowering herbs commonly grown as a pot herb, and it is said:

> *Fine basil desireth it may be her lot,*
> *To grow as the gilliflower, trim in a pot.*

Bush basil produces delicate spicy shrubs whose compact, round form makes them appear naturally topiaried. It was a favorite pot herb for English cottage gardeners, and they would offer it with good wishes to a visiting guest. It is a much better-proportioned potted herb than the more familiar and regal sweet basil, which was considered kingly enough for royal chambers. In fact, the French gave it a sovereign title by referring to it as *herbe royale*.

Another very attractive ornamental basil with long heavy flowering spikes is tree basil (*O. gratissimum*). Grow it as a seasonal standard in a pot, similarly to conservatory plants such as heliotrope or fuchsia.

BAY LAUREL (*Laurus nobilis*)

Although they are technically not herbs, it would be hard to imagine classic French cuisine without bay leaves. The slightly spicy flavor of bay laurel is indispensable in soups, stews, and marinades, but the whole leaves are removed before serving, allowing just the distinctive essence to remain.

Bay laurel is an ancient evergreen shrub or tree of the laurel family, with purple-black berries and leathery, aromatic leaves that take well to formal clipping. In his sixteenth-century herbal, John Gerard noted that bay trees "grow naturally in Spain, where they can reach forty to sixty feet." For those of us who grow them as potted standards in the Northeast, where they must be wintered inside for protection from searing winds and hard frosts, nothing is too much trouble. As a professional herb grower I know once said, "A row of lettuce is a row of lettuce, but a specimen bay tree is a pal." Bay trees bring with them an air of orderliness and a built-in sense of design. Not only do a pair of them add a light-hearted formality to the entrance of your home, but, according to ancient lore, they can be your first line of defense against lightning and thunder as well. Save an honored place in your vegetable garden for a majestic standard of bay laurel, because the evergreen leaves were thought to be a symbol of eternal prosperity. If you're lucky, the tree's potent spirit will guarantee an abundant crop. Moreover, a pair of bay laurel sentries outside the garden gate will ward off witches and wizards.

Bay is a tree of the sun that is native to southern Europe and Asia Minor, and it was dedicated to the Greek sun god Apollo. Legend says that Daphne was loved and pursued by Apollo, who was charmed by the nymph's beauty. One day, as he was about to capture her, she prayed to the gods for help; they took pity on her and turned the mountain nymph into a bay tree. But Apollo's love for her was constant. From that moment on, he wore a wreath of laurel from his sacred tree, and he decreed that poets, victors, and all those who create beauty should be given laurel as their prize. The phrase "Don't rest on your laurels" warns the successful not to lie back on the garlands of their past victories.

In ancient Greece and Rome bay trees provided the leaves for making wreaths to crown winning emperors. However, Julius Caesar, being rather self-conscious about his baldness, sacrificed symbolic honor for vanity by wearing a crown of the larger-leafed *Ruscus racemonsus*. The term "bachelor's degree" is derived from the Latin *bacca-laureus*, meaning "laurel berries," while unmarried men are called bachelors because at one time they were thought to be so absorbed in scholarly pursuits that they avoided marriage for fear of being distracted from their studies.

CHIVES (*Allium schoenoprasum*)

Nothing better announces the end of winter than the sight of little pots of sprightly chives as they first arrive in farmer's markets. For me, their bright green grasslike appearance is the very harbinger of spring. In fact, the herb looks so much like a grass of tiny rushes that it was known as "rush-leek" during the Middle Ages. Chives are a hardy perennial of the *Allium* family, and they are the neatest, prettiest, and most delicate of a group of plants that also includes garlic, shallots, and, of course, onions.

Chives are a very encouraging herb for a beginner to grow, since they develop quickly while their tidy, compact, and hardy nature makes them an ideal potted herb for a kitchen window sill. The clumps tend to grow in 6-inch diameters ranging in height from 6 to 9 inches, although some varieties are more than a foot high. Chives are produced from small white bulbous roots called bulblets, and they are easily propagated by making divisions and replanting a cluster of three to four bulblets to a pot in spring or fall. For those who have an outdoor planting of chives, transplant a clump into a 5-inch pot in late summer and temporarily bury it up to the rim in the ground. After the first frost, loosely mulch the pot with some leaves and pine needles and set it in a cold place for three months, as the herb needs a rest period to rejuvenate. Then bring the pot indoors, putting it in a sunny location, and water it conscientiously. You should have a fresh supply of chives that is ready for harvesting by January. The hollow green leaves are best mowed down like grass with scissors, cutting close to the soil line. This will not only encourage new bulblets to form, but it will keep the thin green growth supple, rather than woody. Feed the plant regularly with diluted fish emulsion after repeated cuttings, in order to replace lost nutrients.

If you are not growing the leaves for harvesting, some of the simplest, prettiest, and most long-lasting of all herb flowers will begin to develop at the top of the spears. The lilac pompoms are a wonderful and unusual addition to arrangements, but I often make small bouquets exclusively from chive flowers that I cut from a couple of pots of a late-summer-blooming variety. As they dry in place, the individual flower heads appear like an enormous pastel pincushion. Clumps of flowering chives make attractive borders for vegetable, herb, and flower gardens. They are good companion plants when grown near roses to combat black spot, as well as discouraging carrot fly and scab infections on apple trees. A strong infusion made of chives is said to prevent mildew when sprayed on gooseberries.

Chives are added to soups and salads when the powerful flavor of onion would be too overwhelming. Use the finely cut leaves in cheese spreads, mashed potatoes, dilled cucumbers, and of course as the classic and necessary addition to sour cream for omelettes. When the thin, wispy leaves are left whole, they will be ribbons of flavor to tie around small bundles of carrot and turnip spears, and they can be used to wrap up bouquets garnis in a charming and tasty way. Marinate the bulblets in a vinaigrette, and serve them as a milder and more delicate form of pickled onions to accompany pâtés and sausages.

DILL (*Anethum graveolens*)

Dill is a poetic weedy annual that is native to southern Europe and Egypt, where it easily self-sows in grain fields. Like parsley and fennel, it is a member of the *Umbelliferae* family, which produces characteristic umbrella-shaped inflorescences. The herb is extremely easy to cultivate, and the prolific seed can be sown directly in pots in March or April. If it is then resown in autumn from the seeds of the original plant, the newer plants tend to be stronger and fuller-flavored. Although the herb resembles fennel in appearance and aroma, it is more suitable for pot culture, as dill seldom has more than a single stalk.

Dill is an ancient herb that was typically found in Greek kitchen gardens growing among the beets, lettuces, and onions. The name is derived from the old Norse word *dilla*, meaning "to dull," and the seeds were given to babies to make them sleep. Perhaps this explains why the Greek herbalist and physician Dioscorides recommended it for nursing mothers in his ancient herbal.

Dill was found both wild and cultivated in Palestine, and it regularly appears under the misnomer "anise" throughout the King James version of the Bible. Confusion has continued to be perpetuated partly because botanists and zoologists were not part of the team of transcribers of this authorized interpretation; and so the apricot that Adam and Eve ate became an apple, the crocodile became a whale, the bull became a unicorn, and dill became anise.

Although the English have cultivated dill as both a garden herb and a potted herb for hundreds of years, it took the irreverent and inspired gardening genius of Vita Sackville-West to incorporate dill decoratively into her twentieth-century flower borders at Sissinghurst. She liked "muddling things up, and if an herb looks nice in a border then why not grow it there?"

The entire plant is aromatic, and, except for the roots, it is all serviceable. You should cut the largest feathery leaves first and use them in vegetable dishes, cheese spreads, and fish preparations like Scandinavian gravlax. I like to use sprigs of delicately flavored dill in homemade soups, rather than the more familiar celery stalks. The French surprisingly and delightfully use the whole seed pod as a tasty addition to some of their cakes, cookies, and pastries.

The seeds resemble those of caraway but are smaller and flatter. To gather them, wait until they darken and then cut the umbels; dry them in the sun and then shake the seeds loose. The whole seed heads, which are prized for pickling and vinegars, prompted Joseph Addison, the eighteenth-century British essayist who often wrote of gardening pleasures, to comment that he so looked forward to the time of year for pickling with dill, but "like the song of the nightingale, it is not heard above two months." So don't expect to grow the greenery in a pot beyond one season; instead, you can enjoy the flavorful seeds throughout the year.

LAVENDER (*Lavendula officinalis*)

The word "lavender" immediately conjures up an aroma or a color; that's how identifiable this herb is and always has been. The genus name, *Lavendula*, comes from the Latin *lavare*, meaning "to wash," and since ancient times lavender has been used for soaps and as a perfuming agent for bath waters. In fact, bathing in it was deemed such a sinfully sensuous experience that its use was condemned  during the Dark Ages. But lavender in all its beauty and fragrance was revived for its cosmetic uses in the late Middle Ages.

The unique aroma of lavender strongly repels insects like flies, moths, and mosquitoes, making it a natural ingredient for sachets, pillows, potpourris, and soaps. In the fourteenth century royal cushions were stuffed with lavender leaves, blossoms, and stems, as all parts of

English lavender (*L. officinalis*) are intensely aromatic. At the same time, the damp floors of houses and churches were strewn with whole branches of this herb in hopes of keeping away plague.

Lavender is an evergreenish-grey perennial herb. It is a shrub in the mint family that was originally native to the dry and undernourished rocky soil of the Mediterranean hillsides, where it was exposed to blazing sunlight and little rainfall. The fine hairs on its leaves, which contribute to the overall greyish hue, also give protection from the cold in the winter and reduce transpiration in the summer. Like the leaves of most textured grey-green plants, lavender's foliage has a tendency to conserve and hold moisture, so one has to be very careful about not overwatering this plant. Lavender prefers a sandy soil with excellent drainage in containerized environments; otherwise it will quickly rot from being left with wet feet. This is a condition that roses also detest, which makes the two natural companions in garden designs. Lavender has crooked, scraggly stems with broomlike spikes composed of whorls of flowers that can be blue-violet, dark purple, pale mauve, pink, and even white, all of which are very attractive to honey-bees and butterflies. In order to retain their aromatic properties, the flowering stems should be harvested just as the florets open.

Perennial lavender can be grown as a flowering shrub in an herbaceous perennial border. Hardy varieties like Hidcote (*L. vera Hidcote*) or Munstead (*L. vera Munstead*) form beautiful grey-green edgings when planted 18 inches on center around an herb garden. Or grow specimen topiaries of lavender in equally pale pots, and punctuate the four corners of a swimming pool with tiers of pompon topiaries grown from the tender perennial French lavender (*L. stoechas*).

Lavender is most definitely the queen of herbs, and, since one can never have too much of a good thing, I grow many varieties as potted herbal topiaries. Northeastern winters are too harsh for these tender perennials, but as potted topiaries they can be brought inside and will do well. One of my favorites is fringed lavender (*L. dentata candicans*), a serrated-edged, greyish lavender whose pale arching leaves are slightly felt-textured. They have a natural curve that gracefully accentuates a rounded form. Like rosemary, it is important to keep this herb well pruned when grown indoors, since the center of the plant can become leafless. Hard pruning in the youthful stages promotes good breaking of branches from the older wood.

To have a specimen lavender topiary waft its fragrance across my rooms is quite romantic. But when summertime comes and I sit on a teak bench surrounded by pots of herbs and watch the honeybees and butterflies dance around a flowering lavender, it's a bit of heaven on earth. No one ever had a more appreciative audience for her good work.

LEMON VERBENA (*Lippia citriodora*)

Lemon verbena is considered the queen of aromatic herbs and no one knows this better than the English, who always adopt a good garden plant when they see one. For nearly 200 years they have integrated lemon verbena so comfortably with their own perennial borders that we've forgotten the plant's true origins.

This is a native American herb that, although short on history and lore, has nevertheless become popular throughout the world, probably because it has the purest and most refreshing aroma of all lemon-scented herbs. In Peru and Central America the plant reaches a height of 12 feet, given warm climates, sandy soil, and protection from wind; but in North America it is a tender perennial garden shrub. It can be grown well in a pot as a mop-headed standard and, because its habit of growth is more relaxed than that of formal bay trees, consider growing lemon verbena standards in ornate terra-cotta jardinières, evenly spaced 5 feet on center through the length of a perennial flower border. The pastel green spheres and clean citrus scent will visually and aromatically unify your garden.

Lemon verbena is a deciduous plant that will probably drop its leaves when it is brought back inside to winter during the colder months. The leaves will reappear, although they will be a little more yellow-green in color. Like most perennial herbs, lemon verbena gains in taste and fragrance, so try to keep the plant from year to year.

The long and thin lancerlike leaves are slightly crinkled and emery-textured. They are arranged in a whorl around the stem. One of the herb's earliest botanical names, *Aloysia triphylla*, describes the characteristic three leaves that grow from each node. (Three-leaf plants were significant in religion because they symbolized the Trinity.) There are small mauve and white clusters of flowers at the end of the branches and, as with any aromatic plant, it is best to harvest the foliage right before it blooms. Because the aroma can linger on the dried leaves for many years, it is invaluable for potpourris, sachets, and teas.

Lemon verbena makes a unique substitute for lemon or mint in poultry, fish, and stuffing recipes. For a special flavor treat add some leaves to fruit salads, lemonade, baked apples, and sponge cakes, or shred it on top of vanilla ice cream.

MARJORAM *(Origanum* species)

William Shakespeare, who must have walked in many herb gardens, did right by marjoram when he immortalized it in Act 4, Scene 5, of "All's Well That Ends Well":

> *Indeed, Sir, she was the sweet marjoram of the salad,*
> *or, rather, the herb of grace.*

Sweet marjoram (*Marjoram hortensis* or *Origanum marjoram*) is sweet in appearance and scent, as well as name. In fact, Venus is said to have created the plant, and it was the touch of her fingers that gave it its sweet perfume. The delicious-smelling leaves create delicate little hedges and borders in mild climates. The herb is a tender perennial of luxuriant growth in its native Portugal, but it must be treated as an annual in the northeastern United States. It produces insignificant white blossoms that are tucked within green knobby growths, sometimes referred to as knots. In Tudor times knotted marjoram, as it was often appropriately called, was one of the few herbaceous plants that were used for edging topiaried knot gardens. Because the herb retains its full flavor and aroma even when dried, it was popularly used in nosegays, dusting powders, sweet bags, washing waters, and for strewing. As a culinary herb, sweet marjoram contributes a wonderful flavor to pâtés, sausages, soups, and stuffings.

The characteristically thick and bushy growth of its leaves and stems made the marjoram plant a good brush or broom, and in the Old Testament a variety of bristly marjoram was used to paint the Israelites' doorposts with the Passover blood so that the angel of death would avoid those houses. Aside from marjoram's functional uses, the carefully tied bundles of dried marjoram and oregano in provincial Mediterranean markets make for some of the sweetest and most beautifully original bouquets imaginable.

There are about thirty varieties of marjoram; all of them are members of the mint family. They will grow from 1½ to 3 feet high, except if they are dwarfed, as they commonly are when found in crevices and walls. Pot marjoram (*Origanum onites* or *Marjorana onites*) is a multi-branching variety that will layer itself into beautiful tufted little mounds or circular clumps and needs frequent cutting back and trimming during the summer. It is slow to germinate from seed, so propagation is usually done with root divisions or layering of offshoots into sandy, well-drained planting mixtures. In addition, pot marjoram needs full sun and shelter from cold wind and, like basil, it also enjoys being watered in midday when it is set outside in the summertime. It has lilac-colored flowers that contribute to the whole plant's reddish hue.

MINT (*Mentha* species)

According to ancient mythology, beautiful young Minta was pursued by Hades, god of the underworld. His enraged wife, Persephone, put a curse on the lovely young nymph and turned her into a humble mint plant that was destined to live on the shady edges of Hades's dark netherworld. But although Minta had lost some of her beauty, her fragrance and freshness would always be very appealing.

The characteristic essential oils that produced mint's strong flavor and refreshing, zestful fragrance were prized by Greeks and Romans for their medicinal value. The clean aroma made it a common strewing herb in Hebrew synagogues, while Persian and Indian cultures hung fragrant sweet bags stuffed with dried mint leaves in their doorways to lend the impression of coolness in hot climates. We have all appreciated the invigorating taste sensation that comes from the menthol content of this plant. It is the very reason that mint extract is popularly used in chewing gums, dentifrices, iced teas, and juleps, as well as often being added to pharmaceutical preparations in order to mask the taste of an unpleasant medication.

Mints grow wild in the Mediterranean area, and the herb's rampant growth makes it appear to have naturalized everywhere. The problem of having it in our own gardens is not how to grow it, but rather how to contain the rapidly spreading underground runners that develop shoots at every joint. Some outdoor gardeners try to gain control over the herb by first planting it in a bottomless pot and then setting it in the soil.

All mints are characterized by squarish stems, purplish flowers that grow in whorls or spikes, and shallow, creeping roots. This last feature makes the perennial herb easily propagated from root divisions or from cuttings taken in early spring from an older plant. Mints like and need a rich, well-watered growing medium. The leaves might tend to yellow if the potting mixture is deficient in nutrients. As it is best to use freshly harvested mint leaves, take comfort in the notion that cutting the plant back will only improve its growth. In fact, letting the flowering stalks go to seed will often do the plant in.

Peppermint (M. *peperita*)

This variety of mint grows to 3 feet high while producing foliage that has an intensely pungent and aromatic taste, actually resembling pepper. Its pointed green oval leaves are commercially distilled to get the finest "oil of peppermint," or menthol. For a nice little treat on a hot summer day, make your own cooling lozenge by sucking on a peppermint leaf wrapped around a cube of sugar.

Spearmint (*M. spicata*)

Spearmint leaves are differentiated from peppermint by their taste and lack of down; they are wrinkled and bright green, and they grow off reddish stems on 2-foot-high plants. Spearmint was originally cultivated in Greece as a preservative for meats, and nowadays it is the most commonly used variety of mint for sauces and jellies that are served with strong-flavored gamy meats and with lamb. This mint is perhaps the most popular flavoring in the world and the most important commercially grown herb.

Catmint or Catnip (*Nepeta cataria*)

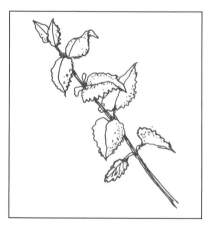

There is a good reason why every Western language contains some variation of the word "cat" in this herb's common name. Catmint is a very pretty plant with downy heart-shaped leaves that will grow almost anywhere. It is often cultivated in English cottage gardens for the soft beauty of its grey-green haze and its equal appeal to all of the local cats. Although it makes an unusual tea, the herb's essential oil is most appreciated by the feline population, and one should definitely grow a pot of it for their fun and pleasure. Here's some propagation advice from William Coles's *Art of Simpling* (1656):

> *If you set it the catts will eate it*
> *If you sow it, the catts won't know it.*

Pennyroyal (*M. pulegium*)

Pennyroyal, one of the most diminutive mints, produces a many-branched, low-growing, glossy mat that is often planted as a garden path. It releases a strong aroma when walked over, while making a good insect repellent that discourages ants. The botanical name comes from the Greek *pulex*, meaning "flea," and at one time this ancient herb was strewn on the floor when food scraps were thrown underneath the table for the dogs, which often carried fleas.

Ancient cultures found many uses for this perennial mint, which is definitely more pungent and less agreeable than most. It was an important ingredient in cleansing unhealthy waters, as well as being a major flavor in barley beverages that were similar to draught beer. It was used to revive people who had fainted, and two sprays tucked behind the ear were believed to prevent heat exhaustion. Because of its long, flexible stems, powerful scent, and profuse blossoms it was not only twisted into wreaths for Greek brides, but the ancient Roman scholar Varro stated unequivocally that a garland of pennyroyal was better for the bedroom than a bower of roses.

Soft cuttings of pennyroyal start well by being pressed into "peat pellets," which are small disks of peat that are held together by polyethylene netting and expand when watered. Or simply press several little strands with their roots intact onto the surface of some potting soil, and keep them evenly moist to encourage successful rooting. The new growth of pennyroyal will make a nice ground cover beneath an herbal topiary if propagated in this manner.

MYRTLE (*Myrtus communis*)

Myrtle is an ancient herb, a Greek symbol of sensual love and passion. Myth has it that Cinyras, a king of Cyprus, was brazen enough to suggest that his daughter Myrrah's beauty rivaled that of Aphrodite, the Greek goddess of love. The jealous Aphrodite took revenge on the lovely Myrrah and consumed her with an incestuous passion for her own father. But when the girl became pregnant with Cinyras's child, Aphrodite took pity on Myrrah and turned her into a myrtle tree; from her gaping trunk sprang forth Adonis, full grown.

With this kind of pedigree it's no wonder that the Athenians rated myrtle berries as one of their four greatest treasures, along with honey, figs, and the propylaea, the splendid gateways to the Acropolis. Myrtle trees were planted around important temples and as sacred groves in Greece and Rome. The berries were regarded as a confection, and people nibbled on them like nuts between banquet courses. They make the breath smell sweet, so they were also used as a natural mouthwash. Myrtle berries produce a wine that was famous for not being intoxicating, and a decoction of myrtle leaves in wine was said to clear up everything from freckles to hangnails. Nowadays several sprigs of myrtle, with their leaves and berries intact, can be used like rosemary to stuff a roast.

Garlands of fresh green myrtle were popular for maidens' flowing tresses, as well as for the more conservative dresser who wanted something less showy than the usual fancy Persian roses. Because it was evergreen and symbolically eternal, the herb was used to crown great thinkers and poets. More recently, Ogden Nash rewarded his own cleverness with garlands in some light verse,

> *Come crown my brows with leaves of myrtle;*
> *I know the tortoise is a turtle.*

The compact myrtle (*M.c. compact*) and the German or dwarf myrtle (*M.c. microphylla*), which has almost needlelike leaves, produce tidy topiary forms. Their interior webbing of brown twigs is uniformly covered by small and fragrant shiny green leaves, from ½ to ¾ inch long. The black berries with purple halos appear after the aromatic cream-colored flowers with fuzzy stamens have come and gone. One of my favorite myrtle topiaries, *M.c. microphylla variegata*, is a true dwarf variety that I've grown for several years. It has small pale green leaves with margins of creamy white, and in the hot summer sunlight it glows with the refreshing translucent color of sparkling lemonade.

Keep architecturally spare settings simple and elegant by planting obelisks of evergreen myrtle in fine old terra-cotta pots. Set them four-square in the center of a courtyard, then take comfort in the notion that myrtle was purported to bring peace and harmony to a home. It is said that a flowering myrtle is one of the luckiest plants to have. And Lady Rosalind Northcote, in her *Book of Herbs*, shares some advice on the secret of its flowering: "While setting the slip [cutting] spread the tail of one's dress and look proud."

Myrtles are handsome subtropical shrubs whose sweet aroma emanates not only from the flowers and leaves but from the bark as well. In fact, myrtle is so sweetly scented that it was thought to be the only herb that Adam brought with him from the garden of Eden. The plant is at home in Greece and the Mediterranean region, and when grown in pots prefers a cool and sunny location.

OREGANO (*Origanum* species)

There is much confusion about oregano and marjoram, as they share interchangeable nomenclature and many of the same characteristics. *Origanum vulgare*, commonly called wild marjoram or winter marjoram, is the perennial marjoram herb in Italy. It is the herb that has become synonymous with pizza seasoning. It is an erect 2-foot-high plant with dull grey-green leaves that are not es-

pecially hairy. Its flowers are pink, white, purple, or lilac-colored. Sprigs of oregano were put on graves in ancient Greece, and if they flowered the dead person was ensured a happy afterlife.

The true oregano, *O. heracleoticum*, is a tender perennial herb that has a dense system of fine roots that produces a low-growing, almost creeping plant with hairy leaves. It has tall flower stalks that grow to 12 inches and yield tiny brown seeds. The plant can be started from seed or cuttings, but it should be harvested as soon as the white flowers appear. Keep in mind that, if the plant is continually cropped, as it should be when grown in a pot, the flowers might never appear. Trim about six weeks after the initial planting, cutting down all shoots to 1 inch from the growing center. This will stimulate dense, bushy new growth. The plant dries quickly without losing its unique properties, due to its "hot" flavor. By rubbing the dried leaves (no stems) through a fine screen you can store oregano for later use as a sprinkling herb.

Oregano is a plant of wide-open spaces, and its Greek name, *origanum*, is derived from *oros*, meaning "mountain," and *ganos*, meaning "joy." In ancient Greece the sight of hillsides covered in the pink and white flowers of oregano did indeed represent "joy of the mountains." In fact, our own state of Oregon takes its name from the oregano that grows there in abundance.

PARSLEY (*Petroselinum* varieties)

Parsley, or *Petroselinum*, grows in rocky locations, and the botanical name is derived from *petros*, the Greek word for "rock" or "stone," while *selinon* is actually the Greek word for "wild parsley." The plant is a hardy biennial, which means it produces flowers and seeds in the second year after germination. But since we are growing parsley primarily for its leaves, we treat the herb as an annual and replant it yearly.

Parsley is most often grown from young plants, as it is very slow to germinate from seed, and an interesting explanation is based on ancient mythology. The plant was dedicated to Persephone, who was queen of Hades and a symbol of spring. Parsley seed was believed to go back and forth nine times to visit the underworld before sprouting, just as Persephone would annually return to the earth for those months that comprised the growing season.

Parsley was indigenous to Crete, and an old Cretan herbal of 1539 suggested stuffing the crisp little parsley seeds into a tennis ball in order to bruise their casings and speed up germination. Nowadays the germination period may be hastened by soaking the seeds in warm water for twenty-four hours before planting.

Keep leaves clipped for thick bushy growth. Harvest often and pick the larger, outermost ones first. As the green and white flower stalks appear, they will make nice herb bouquets on outdoor picnic tables, for the flowers will have to be cut off in any case to preserve the plant's energies.

Because of its early association with death and oblivion, parsley was never brought to the table in ancient Greece, although the Romans popularly ate it on bread for breakfast. Today, parsley is such a commonplace garnish that we tend to overlook its other assets. The herb is rich in vitamins A and B and has more vitamin C than an orange. It is a popular companion plant in vegetable gardens because the decorative leaves are an effective repellent against certain pests.

As to the look of the foliage, Devonshire folklore explains that parsley leaves were torn ragged by enraged pixies, who wanted to punish scoffers for uplifting the tulip beds in order to plant the more utilitarian parsley. After all, everyone knows that tulip cups have always formed the ideal cradle for pixie babies.

There are numerous varieties of parsley ranging from curly moss types (P. crispum) to plain and flat-leaf Italian varieties (P. hortensis) to Hamburg parsley (P. satirum), which has an edible root similar to a small parsnip. Parsley actually belongs to the carrot family, and there is a turnip-rooted variety that produces large and edible roots. The curly-leaf variety grows about 8 inches high, which makes it particularly charming as an edging.

Folklore advises that you plant your parsley every year, even if it proves hardy. It also says, "If the mistress sows the parsley, it always flourishes and so does she." Another bit of wisdom warns, "It takes an honest man to grow parsley well."

ROSEMARY (*Rosmarinus officinalis*)

Rosemary has always been of more significance than any other herb and more important than most of them put together. The name of the herb derives from the Latin words *ros* and *maris*, meaning "dew" or "spray from the sea"; *officinalis* designates a plant that had some commercial value and that was listed in the official pharmacopoeia. Along with ivy, myrtle, and bay, rosemary was one of the most frequently used evergreen plants in Roman gardens and actually was encouraged to climb all over the surrounding walls. The herb thrives in a cool climate tempered with salt winds from the sea. It will survive the winter when planted in pots if the roots—said to be the most tender part of the plant—are kept from freezing.

It is usually recognized as having one species, *R. officinalis*, but there are many interesting varieties, distinguished by color of flowers or habit of growth. *R.o. roseus* has lilac-pink flowers fading to mauve in the bright sun, while *R.o. albus* has white flowers.

A standard of *R.o. prostratus* will create a unique weeping tree whose branches cascade down like a blue waterfall when it is in flower. *R.o. augustifolium* has a pine-needle scent and, when grown like a small fastigiated evergreen, makes a perfect topiaried Christmas tree for a small apartment. It will become fuller and more cherished from year to year. Plant it in an old rose pot of mellowed terra cotta; decorate it only if you must, with the tiniest red glass balls. And on Christmas eve, underplant it with a "mulch" of Lilliputian gifts.

Keeping rosemary pot-bound not only adds to the strength of its fragrance but is said to encourage flowering as well. Charming, aromatic, small blossoms that are most often a clear blue color rivaling that of cornflowers grow on the new wood for many weeks. For this lovely reason, try to schedule your pruning in summertime after the plant has bloomed. Because the flowers are said to intoxicate bees, rosemary was used as a forage at a time when honey was vital to ancient diets. Remembering its origins, rosemary needs good drainage, doing best in sandy soils, and will tolerate no less than two hours of daily sun indoors during winter's shortest days. Although rosemary can withstand a drought in its natural habitat, I have occasionally lost a potted plant by missing a crucial watering.

Rosemary was an herb that followed you from cradle to grave. A sprig was used to stir cups at christenings, while during the courting season its wood was made into lutes for lovers' madrigals. It is linked with remembrance and affection; young Greek and Roman couples wore woven wreaths of rosemary on their wedding day. In the seventeenth century sprigs of gilded rosemary were dipped into scented waters and distributed to wedding guests, symbolizing love and faithfulness. The bridesmaids presented the groom with a beribboned bunch of rosemary, and the bridal bouquet always held an individual sprig as an omen of a happy marriage. Perhaps the wedding banquet even featured fowl stuffed with rosemary's highly flavorful branches.

Its pungently aromatic and somewhat camphoraceous odor made rosemary a necessity in clothes chests to ward off moths and other insects. The herb was used in funeral rites because of its potentially fumigating aroma, and fresh branches were customarily placed in the hands of the dead. Often the shoots rooted, and, when the coffins were later opened, the corpses were fully decked out in rosemary.

This herb has always been a symbol of friendship, and I like to tuck a fresh little sprig in my letters.

SAGE (*Salvia officinalis*)

Sage has always been renowned for its health-giving properties. It was considered so valuable that the Chinese traded 3 pounds of tea leaves for 1 pound of dried sage leaves. Greek physicians held sage to be sacred because of its healing powers. The botanical genus name, *Salvia*, is derived from the Latin *salvere*, which means "to be in good health." Ultimately, to be a "sage" was to have the wisdom and knowledge of healing.

The plant belongs to the mint family, and it is native to southern Europe, where it grows abundantly on the hillsides of Yugoslavia's Dalmatian coast. But one variety of the herb, *S. judaica*, grew on the mountains of Palestine and, according to a description in the Old Testament, the branched inflorescences of this lowly plant inspired the form of the multilimbed candlestick that became the traditional Jewish menorah.

Like most herbs that are native to the Mediterranean, sage will do best in light soil and a warm, sunny location. Although the plant is a hardy biennial, it starts to degenerate while growing in a pot, so it should be replanted yearly. This is done very easily from seeds (which are not unusually tiny), layerings, root divisions, or cuttings taken from the outermost shoots of the plant.

Although *Salvia officinalis* was the species listed in the official pharmacopoeia, there are more than 500 species of *Salvia* and dozens of varieties with differing colors, leaf shapes, and life cycles. Sage has culinary, chemical, medicinal, horticultural, and decorative uses. The plant can grow to a height of 4 feet, as in the Vatican strain of *S. sclarea*, whose popular name, clary, refers to its ability "to clear the eyes." It makes a beautiful and impressive potted herb, especially if it is set against other tall mauvey-blue flowering perennials like delphiniums. Its aroma is also a very welcome contrast to the surrounding sweeter-scented plants. The colors of sage range from the "Wild West's" *S.o. purpurascens*, made famous by Zane Grey's *Riders of the Purple Sage*, to the more familiar and tranquil grey-green of meadow sage (*S. pratensis*).

The strong-tasting sage seeds were used as a savory in the rather bland cheeses of ancient Rome, and to this day sage-flavored cheeses are processed in Derbyshire. The herb was also widely served as sage fritters or "frytures," which were big hits as finger food at medieval banquets. For our own contemporary feasting, sage has virtually become the national Thanksgiving herb, as its wrinkly, flavorful leaves are traditional stuffing for holiday turkeys.

SANTOLINA (*Santolina chamaecyparissus*)

Santolina was one of the most decorative medieval herbs, and, along with boxwood and wall germander, it became one of the three most popular choices for outlining herb gardens. It is sometimes referred to as cotton lavender, although santolina is not a lavender but rather a member of the daisy family. The whitish-green leaves are serrated along their edges, creating a dazzling haze in bright sunlight, where the plant grows best. It thoroughly enjoys hot locations in sandy soils that are protected from wind. Without these conditions the decorative herb becomes woody and the foliage deteriorates into a greyish, crumbling mess. Santolina likes pruning, and its prissy neatness originally made it perfect for fussy rims on dainty Victorian tussie-mussies and as refined edgings around herb gardens.

Santolina is easily propagated from cuttings taken as the plant starts to grow in the spring. If it is clipped back at this time it will produce decorative little lemon-clustered buttons in the summertime. The flowering stems should always be removed to keep the plant full. Both the leaves and flowers have a pungent aroma that made the herb popular as a fumigant against moths. In France it was also called *garde de robe*, having once been laid in winter wardrobes and chests to protect against insects.

Santolina is most effective in garden design when it unifies individual silver-grey plants while casting a resplendent sheen of its own. When clipped into tiers of pompons or fastigiated cones, it forms beautiful pastel-hued topiaries. In my seaside herb garden I grow it as a miniature hedge whose color and texture mimic the sea foam. Every 5 feet the border is punctuated by a vertical cone of santolina. Rescaled to my own herb garden, it recalls the classic walls of cypress that surround Mediterranean villas in the south of France, and I was delighted to discover that the French once referred to santolina as *petit cyprez*.

SCENTED-LEAF GERANIUMS
(*Pelargonium* species)

Eleanour Sinclair Rohde was an English gardener earlier in this century. Her scholarly research, written in the most pleasurable prose, makes her my favorite practical and romantic writer on herbs. Of scented-leaf geraniums she says, "My own first recollections of sweet-leaved geraniums go back to the days when as a child I used to stay with my Great-Aunt Lancilla. The light came pouring in through the sloping glass roof and there was a whole bank of the scented-leaf geraniums, reaching well above my head. Pinching the leaves was always a joy for the scents were so rich and varied."

Scented-leaf geraniums are both ancient herbs and old-fashioned garden favorites. Their major attractions are their scents, which have been used for ingredients in potpourris, soaps, and perfumes. They comprise a vast assortment of intriguing foliage plants that reached the height of popularity during the nineteenth century. The ability of their leaves to mimic other aromas suggested hidden meanings and private messages, to the delight of Victorian gardeners.

The genus name *Pelargonium* comes from the Greek *pelargos* meaning "stork," while "geranium" is a modification of the Greek *geranion*

unlike any other herb in its strong yet sweet aroma, should be considered as a culinary herb in your garden.)

French tarragon is considered one of the "fine herbs," as opposed to the "robust herbs." It adds delicious interest to a humble chicken salad, gives a definite flavor to white cider vinegar, and is an essential ingredient in a classic French *béarnaise*, which is my favorite sauce with white-meat fish like sole or pink-flesh meat like lamb.

Interestingly, French tarragon, unlike Russian tarragon, can be propagated only vegetatively, as it does not produce seed. It is one of the few instances in which a sterile but horticulturally superior variety of a garden herb has been spread throughout the world by vegetative propagation. And so it becomes an herb gardener's pleasant duty to continue to divide the plant and pass along its goodness.

Separate and cut the roots into short but substantial clumps, according to my earlier instructions. Transplant the individual clusters into 10-inch pots, allowing plenty of room for tarragon's rangy root growth. The herb prefers a poor, rather sandy, soil and will tolerate less than full sun. If you are careful not to overwater it while indoors and if you feed it twice a month, tarragon will do fine in pot culture. Since tarragon is very easy to handle and the flavor only deteriorates with age, keep several potted plants at different stages of growth. This will enable you to divide and replant this herb on a rotation system without ever lacking a pot of it.

THYME (*Thymus* species)

Thyme is another ancient herb. Its tiny purple blossoms have colored the slopes of Greece for millennia. The perfumed air of wild thyme is as familiar to the Greek countryside as the scent of lavender is to the landscape of Provence.

Thyme can be green, grey, or golden. Its tiny leaves (only ³⁄₁₆ inch long by ¹⁄₁₆ inch wide) can be woolly, shiny, or silver-edged. Thyme can

make up a whole lawn or a trail between stepping stones; it will carpet hillsides and upholster garden love seats.

The genus *Thymus* includes possibly 100 species and even the Royal Horticultural Society admits that thymes are notoriously difficult to classify and identify. *Thymus* is a derivation from the Greek *thymum*, meaning "to burn" or "to sacrifice," as the herb was originally used in sacrificial ceremonies to the gods. The powerful incense of such varieties as camphor (*T. camphoratus*), turpentine (*T. comosus*), and varnish (*T. jankae*) was thought to have the ability to drive away diseases and annoying insects. It was a common strewing herb in medieval times, to be put down against plague, and it was essential to every well-stocked stillroom. Oil of thyme or thymol, was used extensively as a battlefield antiseptic in World War I and even today this substance is added to cough drops, mouthwashes, and toothpastes as an antiseptic. A bunch of thyme was often collected and dried while still in flower and always seemed to be hanging near the kitchen hearth.

Thyme is the favorite herb of bees, and in ancient Greece the little leaves were rubbed over the hives as a lure and to guarantee a profuse honey crop. The herb produces the distinct flavor in the honey of Mount Hymettus, said to be the finest in the world. It was also a common practice to plant thyme as a ground cover in Mediterranean orchards to encourage butterflies and other insects to pollinate the fruit trees.

Today we mainly grow two groups of thyme in our herb gardens. *T. serpyllum*, from the Greek meaning "to creep along," is also called wild thyme or mother-of-thyme. This species includes a large number of individual varieties of prostrate thymes that grow in bumpy mounds forming small, tufted little cushions. *T. vulgaris*, or common thyme, is a perennial herb more often grown for culinary than for decorative purposes.

Thyme is one of the most important herbs in cooking, to be used almost as freely as salt and with a lot less fear. It is an essential ingredient in the blend of herbs called a bouquet garni. More delicate than sage, thyme has a flavor that enhances stews, and it is perfect with red meat, poultry, fish, and vegetables. It makes a wonderful addition to clam chowders, eggs, and cheese dishes, as well as salad greens.

Thyme is essential to every herb garden, but it is tough to grow into an upright standard since most varieties would rather lie low. Nevertheless, I was determined to find a thyme that might shape up for pot culture, and I came across a camphor thyme in a nursery that had escaped the mass pruning shears; instead of being uniformly cut back, it had the beginnings of a dominant central lead. I continued to encourage branching at the top, and ultimately I had a rounded head of tiny thyme leaves. The precious little topiary is sitting pretty on top of a short gnarly stem that never needed a support stake, and all of the elements are in perfectly scaled harmony.

Thyme is said to rob the soil of nutrients, so occasionally scratch some Electra into the top of the pot. Feed regularly with diluted fish emulsion when the plant is in a period of active growth. Remembering its origins, thyme likes full sun and a light, dry, stony, or sandy soil; according to ancient Greek wisdom, its taste is enhanced by breezes of sea air.

VICTORIAN ROSEMARY
(Westringia rosmariniformis)

An interesting decorative plant for topiary, *Westringia rosmariniformis* was popular in Victorian conservatories; because it resembled *Rosmarinus officinalis*, it was referred to as Victorian rosemary. It is a plant in the mint family and native to Australia and Tasmania. The blue-green leaves with silvery undersides grow in a whorl, circling the individual stems and producing a compact and bushy shrub that is perfect for shaping.

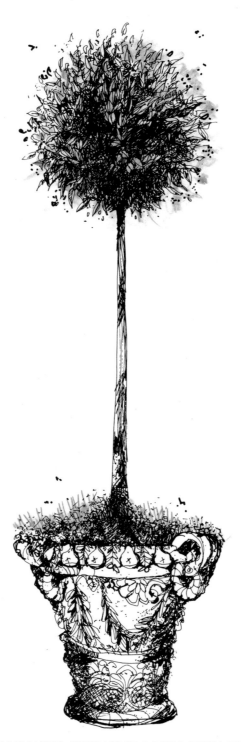

A 6-FOOT BAY LAUREL STANDARD IN A DELLA ROBBIA JARDINIERE

HERBAL TOPIARIES

ll topiary work requires much care and labor; but wherever it appears, whether in a single tree or in an elaborate series of gardens, it rewards the gardener with a peculiar sense of satisfaction; it is witness to the thought and time expended on it, it weds the garden to the human fancy, and is one of the fullest and most delightful embodiments of garden architecture."

Walter H. Godfrey wrote this passage in his small volume *Gardens in the Making* (1914). His aim was to make clear the possibilities that lie as much in the smallest plot as in larger grounds. Today we have even less time and space for our gardening, but there is always room for a garden of potted herbs.

I've been told that my groupings of herbal topiaries, set in front of my windows against the backdrop of Central Park, evoke miniature forests and scaled-down versions of the fairy-tale gardens of the world. How amusingly these simple green shapes play with our perceptions of reality. Yet the very real world of gardening is about creating fantasies and magical experiences, and, while potted topiaries make an unusually lovely indoor herb garden, they ultimately provide a form of enchantment in a world that can always use some make-believe.

Topiary is an art and a craft. It involves forming and clipping trees and shrubs into sculptured shapes, anything from whimsical follies to green architecture to the charm of potted herbs. William Lawson, a down-to-earth sixteenth-century writer of books on everyday gardening, said that topiary was "seeing what nature corrected by art could do." And Gertrude Jekyll, the gifted twentieth-century English artist more famous for her contribution to the art of perennial flower gardens, believed that topiary was "growing things as a means of expression in that domain of design that lies between architecture and gardening."

Through centuries and civilizations, in every land and every culture, the art and craft of topiary has been practiced, praised, and condemned. For those who might too quickly criticize all topiary for being out of harmony with nature, remember that originally people grew things just to survive. Gardening evolves into pleasurable and aesthetic pursuits only after the necessity of growing plants for food has been satisfied.

I am no more interested in ruthless attempts at mastery over nature or grandly artificial designs than Joseph Addison, a British essayist and poet of the early eighteenth century, who had seen Versailles and with quiet denunciation said, "I was not impressed." My own inspiration comes from the utilitarian charm of the small topiaried medieval herb gardens. Historically these were some of the most appealing and appropriate designs from nature's greenery.

HOW TO GROW A STANDARD

All around the world, trees are the subject of legends and lore, proverbs, and folktales. The simple silhouette of a topiary standard brings to mind a childlike drawing of a tree. The shape becomes an icon, imbued with its own powerful symbolism. A standard represents a tree, which symbolizes life; that is why trees are often planted at a baby's birth. A topiary standard is composed of a round head. This roundness is the perfect form. It represents the whole. It is the universe set above a spine or staff, like the world being supported by Atlas.

Any plant can become a standard, be it a rose, an annual, or an herb, if grown as a busy head above a single stem. Good perennial herbs for topiary are rosemary, myrtle, bay laurel, santolina, scented-leaf gera-niums, lavender, and lemon verbena. Perennial herbs are lush plants that thrive on pruning and poor soil, two conditions that you should have no trouble providing. And because herbs feature little leaf forms, the end result of an herbal topiary standard will resemble a miniature tree, with all of its elements in correctly scaled-down proportion.

"A twig in time becomes a tree." That's a Latin American proverb and the simplest description of how to make a topiary standard. Here's a little more help.

Use a healthy and bushy perennial stock plant that is in active growth and has been watered a couple of hours earlier to ensure that the tissues are full of moisture. Select several straight, semihard shoots that show promising new growth for your vegetative stem cuttings. Always take leafy cuttings, not ones with flower buds or part of the flower stalk.

6-week old rooted cutting   at 3 months   at 6 months

Make the cutting just below a leaf joint, or node. It should be from 3 to 5 inches long with several leaves along the stem. Include some of the soft greenish branch as part of the cutting, which represents the current season's growth; this will make the cutting more likely to root. Hardwood herb cuttings will often not root as easily, if at all.

Cut with a sharp downward stroke of a knife, going through the branch at a slight angle. Do not use scissors, which will pinch the tissues of the stem together and make it more difficult for roots to form. It is wise to take several cuttings to be on the safe side, as well as being more interesting and exciting for the grower. Make them all of a uniform length, but don't check the growth of the parent plant by pruning too vigorously. If the cutting is full of sap, set it aside in an upright position for a couple of hours so that the cut end heals over, while keeping the leaves covered with a moist towel. Otherwise a cutting should be planted as soon as possible so that it is not needlessly stressed by wilting.

Carefully remove the bottommost leaves along the stem, those that would wind up below the soil line. Do not cut off the lateral branches, but keep them pinched in order to force the growth into the main stem and help it to thicken up.

Fill a 3-inch clay pot with a growing medium of two-thirds sand and one-third perlite. Pack it well, water it thoroughly, and allow it to drain. Soil and peat moss are eliminated from the rooting mixture in order to have maximum drainage, as the cutting is most susceptible to rot at this point without having a root system to absorb the water. Lightly brush the end of the stem with a commercial hormone powder, preferably one fortified with a fungicide. Using a chopstick or a pencil, pierce a hole down through the mix, making the opening a little bit wider than the stem of the cutting. Insert the stem about 1 inch into the medium, being careful not to wipe off the hormone powder. Firm the moist growing mixture around the little cutting so that the cutting is not loose or shaking. Carefully water from the top, bringing the soil into close contact with the base of the stem.

Place the cutting in bright but filtered sunlight; setting the cutting in direct sunlight will cause it to transpire and rot. Keep the rooting medium moist, never letting it dry out. Mist every morning and only in the morning; since the cutting does not yet have any roots to absorb moisture, misting at night would keep the environment too wet, encouraging fungus and causing rot.

Check for roots in about three weeks: if you tug lightly and the cutting pulls back, some roots have formed. Once the cutting is rooted, fill a 4-inch pot with a light planting medium of equal parts of soil, peat moss, sand, and perlite to which has been added a half-teaspoon of superphosphate or Electra for nourishment and transfer the rooted cutting to this pot.

A standard-in-training topiary must have positive reinforcement right from the start. Firmly anchor a 24-inch bamboo stake alongside the stem, and push it down to the bottom of the pot. Gently tie the stem and stake together with ultrathin wisps of raffia all along the length. Take care not to emboss an impression into the soft growing tissue. If raffia or twine cuts into a plant's trunk or limbs, it will produce a girdling effect that makes unsightly ridges. This is never desirable.

Within a few weeks the cutting will start to grow. Since you must always consider the future proportion of your topiary standard, now is the time to make your plans. Allow the stem, which is fast becoming a "trunk," to grow some distance even though it will look quite spindly and silly at this point. Remember it's just at the gangling adolescent stage.

If you root your cutting in early summer, the stem growth will occur during the shortening daylight hours. This can be used to the topiary's advantage. As the stem reaches for the light it will naturally stretch, or etiolate, a condition that is ordinarily undesirable for indoor plants. Professionals use a form of gibberellin, a growth hormone, which is injected into the plant or applied to the soil around the roots. This substance increases the distance between the nodes along the trunk, making the plant grow taller quicker. This is then counteracted by a chemical retardant, paclobutragol, which reduces the internodal length. A window-sill gardener can gain length in the trunk with a lot less horticultural hocus-pocus.

When the trunk reaches the height you want it to be, it is essential to stop the unlimited upward growth and begin to develop the topiary's form. Carefully start pinching off the lower leaves, but allow 2 inches of leaf growth to remain at the top, leaving five or six branches. This will become the future topiary's head and enable it to carry on photo-

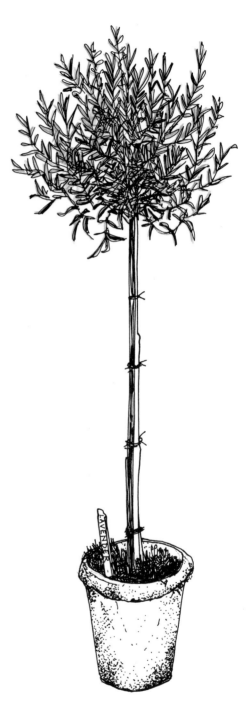

at 14 months

A 2-year-old Topiary Standard

synthesis. Multiple branching will be encouraged if you continue to pinch out the growing tips, and eventually a round and bushy head will take shape.

Correct proportion is critical to the design of a standard. The bay laurel trees that grace the White House are 5 feet high so that the trunk is in a more ideal proportion to heads that are formed of larger leaves. I have seen flowering standards of mop-headed heliotrope that are 7 feet high, gracing the air with their heady fragrance. I prefer elegantly proportioned plants, and I would not start a round-headed topiary before having at least 10 to 12 inches of stem growth.

Plants should be "potted on," or moved to a larger pot, when the roots outgrow their present container. If you seem to be watering daily, the pot has probably become filled with roots and there is little or no soil to retain the moisture. Before repotting, water the plant well, as a dry soil will cling to the pot's sides and not allow the root ball to slide out easily. (The root ball is the mass of roots and potting compost formed by a plant in a pot or other contained situation.) Remove the plant from the container with its root ball intact by upending the pot and gently knocking the rim on a hard surface while holding your other hand across the soil line. The plant should fall neatly into your palm. Loosen and remove some of the compressed soil from around the root ball by tickling the roots free.

You can now transplant your topiary into a clean 6-inch clay pot, which will be its home for some time. Include a shallow bottom layer of pebbles for good drainage. You might at this same time add a second half-height stake to help maintain the verticality of the new trunk. Replant the topiary deep enough to ensure that the surface of the soil will be a little below the new soil line. Crumble fresh soil around the plant, firming it while filling up the pot, and follow with a thorough watering. Retamp and add more soil if needed. Water one more time and do not water again until the plant dries out and then only when needed. Do not start fertilizing until the herb has adapted to its new home and is putting out lots of fresh green growth.

THE ART AND PLEASURE OF PRUNING

It happens every morning, when I should perhaps be starting the day in another way. I become distracted by giving one of my little green conceits a long overdue haircut and all else can just wait. I know a professional grower who will return to his greenhouses after a grueling eighteen-hour day, and, forgetting his weariness, will pick up a favorite pair of pruners. Easily but thoughtfully he will start to trim the most enchanting group of unkempt green soldiers. Before him stand ranks of potted herbal topiaries, each one tall and straight and waiting for its regimental haircut. "Sometimes," he says, "I feel more like a barber than a horticulturist."

For him, pruning his potted topiaries at the end of a demanding day is perhaps a comfortable way to restructure his world. I do this very same thing just as the sun is rising to set an order and clarity in my own head that, I hope, will be with me for the rest of my day.

Most amateurs resist pruning because the growth of a plant is a sign of their good work. They figure, "Why fool around with success?" Right? Wrong! All plants should be pruned as they grow. It is a part of regular care, just like watering and fertilizing. Pruning energizes dormant buds; it is essential to a strong well-balanced plant. All trees, shrubs, and plants benefit by growth control, and topiary simply uses the healthy advantages of pruning to create a specific effect or form.

Because you are master of the plant's design, its growth can be very self-consciously directed with your pruners. Just remember the prudent

advice of Nathaniel Lloyd, creator of Great Dixter, one of England's finest topiary gardens. In his seminal work on topiary, *Garden Craftsmanship in Yew and Box* (1925), he advises that "*Festina lente*" ("make haste slowly") should be the motto of the topiarist. "It is better to cut away less than what is anticipated necessary and to go over the area a second time, than to risk cutting too much and have to wait several years to make good the error."

Tools

The right tool makes all the difference in the success and enjoyment of your gardening. My favorite tool for pruning herbal topiaries is a pair of so-called combination kitchen and garden shears, which can be bought at any well-stocked housewares store. The impulse-hardened blades make them tough enough to cut through thin woody stems, yet they are fine for general shearing and detailed pruning as well. Their wide rabbit ears have a PVC coating that can be used comfortably for long periods without causing finger cramps.

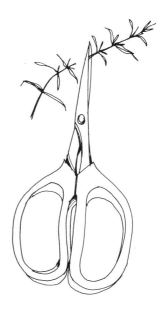

Regular Pruning

It is important to give your topiary regular "haircuts" in the earliest stages of growth in order to develop the initial shape. Securely position the potted topiary at eye level, and try to do your pruning against a solid white background so that the silhouette is clearly defined. Always hold the tip of the pruners in the direction that you want the form to grow and the cutting blades will follow. Work on one side of the plant at a time, and keep rotating the pot as you clip off unwanted growth; eventually you will have completed the whole shape. When pruning a round form, set the potted topiary back on ground level and stand over the plant so that you can use the circumference of the pot as a cutting guide.

Put a drop cloth of newspapers around the base of the plant and you

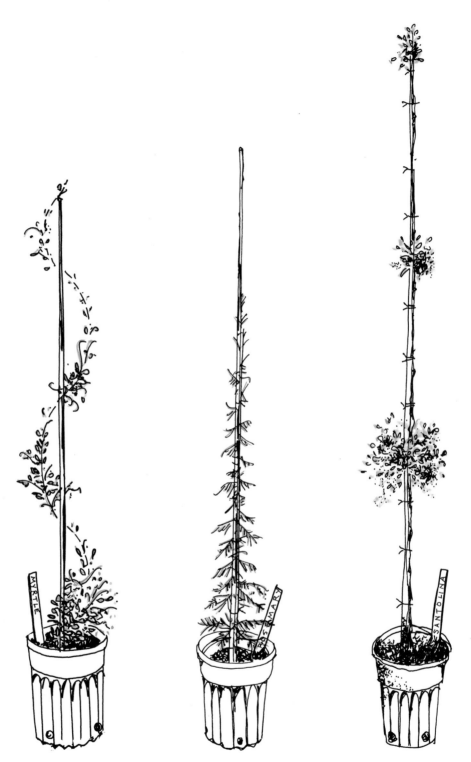

14-month-old Myrtle spiral, Rosemary cone, and Santolina Pom-pon Topiaries

72

probably won't have any sweeping up to do later on. When you've finished pruning but before lifting the drop cloths, dislocate any loose cuttings by holding the stem of the plant and giving it a good but gentle shake. Use tweezers to pick out remaining dead interior leaves.

Radical Pruning

It is sometimes necessary to prune a plant drastically in order to correct for a broken limb, sunburn, or wind damage, or negligent watering patterns, all of which might have caused loss of foliage and made for a distorted topiary shape. If possible, try to do this kind of pruning in an active growing season. Cut the topiary plant back very severely, right into the hardwood, but you must leave some stems with green growth. Radical pruning should force the plant to put out lots of new shoots, which will eventually fill in the distortion. You will be able to retrain your topiary form from the new growth, which might even suggest another shape for you to try. If the plant can be placed outside in bright sunlight during the recovery stage, so much the better; otherwise, set it in your very sunniest window.

Root Pruning

Ideally a plant's head and root growth should remain in proportion. You do not want a pot full of roots supporting some miserly branches any more than a few forlorn roots can be made to nourish and sustain a mass of top growth.

In addition to cutting back the above-ground growth, it is good horticultural practice to do minor root pruning occasionally. This allows a well-developed plant to continue living in the same treasured pot. Perhaps once a year, at the end of a period of dormancy, you can carefully remove the plant from its pot and slice off ½ inch of soil from around the root ball with a sharp knife. Give the plant a gentle shake, add some friable new soil to the pot, and then return the plant to its original home. Water it well and put it in a light but not sunny window. After several weeks the herb will have stabilized; move it to a sunnier location when it starts to acknowledge your good deed by producing new green growth all over.

It is important to understand that pruning should never be approached as a chore. Clipping herbs can be the most pleasurable kind of pruning, as your shears move from plant to plant releasing the sweet smell of myrtle, the clean spicy aroma of lavender, the citrus scent of lemon verbena. Do it when you are inspired and have enough time that you don't feel pot-bound. If you garden in haste, you will repent at leisure. Pruning herbs is a quiet and relaxing pleasure; you get involved with their calmness. It is a thoughtful process that can be peaceful and inspiring—at times even meditative—and, if done with the right karma, it will reward not only the plants but the grower as well.

OTHER SIMPLE TOPIARY SHAPES

Success breeds success, and once you've rooted your first cuttings, all kinds of herbal topiary seem possible. Just remember:

1. *Keep it simple and clear. Capture your topiary shape by eliminating the details and concentrating on the wholeness of the piece.*

2. *Exaggerate the essence of your topiary form. Make it bold and solid-looking.*

3. *Prune accurately. The appeal of all topiary work lies in its ability to conjure up an image that is described in greenery. "Much of the charm of topiary is owed to the accuracy with which they've been trimmed," says Nathaniel Lloyd.*

Your individual topiaries are small green creatures that possess personalities of their own, like any other living pet. You will come to appreciate this and best enhance their individual charms as you work with them.

Day by day and year by year you are growing green designs that will afford as much pleasure in their early stages as in their perfected forms. Simple herbal topiaries will have a shape in less than a year, and they will start to ripen in less than three years. That's no time compared to outdoor formal topiary gardens, which might attain perfection only long after they were planted.

Here are some other basic designs that are perfect for potted herbal topiaries.

Mopheads or Mushrooms

Mopheads are grown like a standard, but their head is a modified half-circle; when grown on short trunks, they might look like mushrooms. They are made from plants such as myrtle, bay laurel, and varieties of lavender, which do not send out branches in all directions. The exaggerated sloping sides of the dome provide greater surface area for leaf activity, and will prevent the head from becoming a twiggy and distorted circle.

Cones

Tonsiled topiaries are like exclamation marks. Their verticality attracts the eye in our horizontal landscapes. Cones are almost easier to start than standards; it's just a matter of keeping the central lead growing. This lead, or leader, is the vertical continuation of the trunk, which, if left to its own devices, will continue to grow upward and onward indefinitely. The most important rule of thumb with any topiary that begins at the base of a pot is to begin with a very full cutting or plant. Nathaniel Lloyd says, "It may be laid down as an axiom that it takes two to three times as long to grow a good base to a plant, as to fill in at the top."

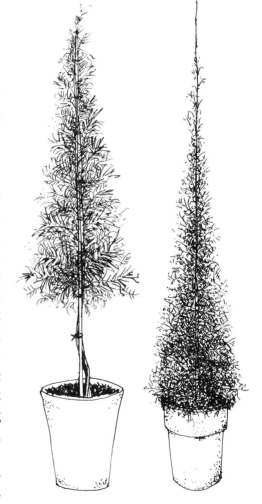

Use an herb plant of rosemary, myrtle, lavender, or santolina that features a prominent lead and shows bushy growth down to the soil line. Carefully insert a stake alongside the stem that is the ultimate height of your planted topiary. Anchor the lead to the stake with thin raffia ties, and continue to encourage the lead up along the stake. Pinch out any errant tip growth that does not conform to the cone's shape, but do not prune off any side branches. Make the bottom of the cone the same width as the rim of the pot and gradually shear the sides up to a thin elegant taper. You can stop the vertical growth at any point by cutting the lead. If you later decide to have a taller cone, simply re-create a new leader by bending up the longest nearby branch and aligning it with the trunk. Secure it to a tall new stake and continue to grow it on as before. This can be done each time you want to increase the height of a cone topiary. In fact that's exactly how a charming 15-inch-high cone of pine-needle rosemary became my perennial 4-foot Christmas tree.

Tetrahedrons

Tetrahedrons were very popular garden forms during the sixteenth century, the Golden Age of Topiary. In effect they were the pyramids of the eighteenth century. They are started like cones but have either three or four sides that are sheared into flat planes. Try to create an elegant "batter," which is the slope from the ground inward toward the top of the plant. It will be easier to define the crisp edge of your form by using small-leafed herbs such as myrtle and numerous varieties of scented-leaf geraniums.

Spirals

These spirited whirling dervishes provoke the most-often-asked question in topiary design, "Does it really grow that way?" Spirals are the essence of topiary follies. They can add a smile to somber gardens without being cute or comical.

Use a one-year-old cutting that features a strong vertical lead. Do not remove any side leaf or lateral branch formations, and don't prune back the top growth either. Start to spiral the flexible young cutting around a strong bamboo stake that has been positioned in the soil right next to the stem. Envision the individual diagonal layers of the coiled form, and continue to shape it through pruning. The mature effect should have each layer sitting tightly above the preceding one, exposing as little trunk between them as possible. Prune and encourage the form to look fluffy and substantial.

Taper the spiral by making it wider at the base and diminishing to a slender graceful twirl at the top. The form should express the natural growth of the plant, which narrows and exhausts its strength in its upward thrust. Spiral topiaries are best made from tight and bushy herbs like santolina, myrtle, and westringia.

Pompons

A tier of these globes is nothing more than starting the lowest level of a standard topiary while choosing a lead and letting it grow through the round form and along a stake. Allow this lead to branch out and get bushy, while still refining the lower sphere. From the upper head choose another lead and let that one grow and be developed into either a sphere, a cone, or an arrowhead. Leave enough breathing space between each level to develop good-size rounds so that they are not pinched together when they reach their final proportion. Use rosemary, westringia, myrtle, santolina, lavender, or bay laurel to create tiers of pompons.

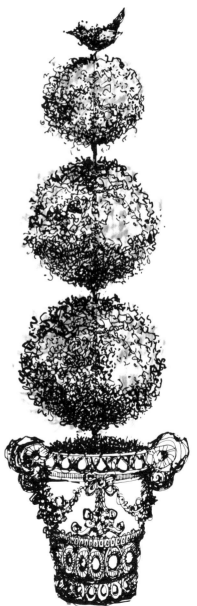

DECORATE ALL YOUR FOOD PREPARATIONS WITH HERBAL CUTTINGS

SIMPLY DELICIOUS

 n our very busy lives, what could be a more generous gesture to your guests than to prepare a simple addition to your meal? It will lend a delicious quality that no professional chef or take-out food shop can duplicate. Here is a collection of easy enticements that are quickly elevated to small gastronomic luxuries by the creative use of herb cuttings. Since potted herbs provide a year-round crop, think of these recipes whenever you're pruning.

Here are two nibbling treats that are specialties of Provence, where herbs are the background scenery and foreground flavor.

THYME-FLECKED BLACK OLIVES

Fill a stoneware crock with tiny black olives. Marinate for a week in fine olive oil, coarse salt, bay leaves, chopped rosemary, a strip of orange peel, and a handful of thyme leaves. Serve with aperitifs.

LAVENDER SWIZZLE STICKS

Make a dainty confection from whole sprigs of just-picked lavender blossoms. Beat 3 egg whites and ¼ cup of sugar until frothy. Dip the lavender sprigs into the mixture to coat them. Set aside to dry for 2 hours on a sheet of nonstick parchment paper. Serve with after-dinner espresso.

BOUQUET GARNI

This is a little bundle of herbs, specifically two parsley sprigs, one bay leaf, and a small branch of thyme, for flavoring soups, stews, sauces, braised meats, and vegetables. The herbs are tied together in order to simplify their removal from a dish at the end of the cooking process. Although they are usually bound with some kitchen twine, why not tie the bouquet with a twist of chives. If dried herbs are used, put them in a square of cheesecloth, and likewise gather and tie it closed with some strands of chives.

For a less than classic and slightly more spirited mixed herb bouquet, consider adding some sage and mint leaves.

CHICKEN JOINTS WITH ROSEMARY SAUCE

Consider making batches of deliciously flavored chicken wings and thighs for picnics or parties.

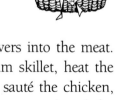

1 pound small chicken wings or thighs
2 cloves garlic, peeled and slivered
1 cup flour, seasoned with salt and freshly ground pepper
2 tablespoons butter
8 tablespoons walnut oil
juice of 1 lemon
2 tablespoons honey
1 tablespoon fresh rosemary leaves, chopped
½ lemon, very thinly sliced
sprigs of rosemary for garnish

Delicately slit the chicken skin and wedge garlic slivers into the meat. Dredge the joints in the seasoned flour. In a medium skillet, heat the butter and oil over high heat until sizzling. Quickly sauté the chicken, turning and browning on all sides. Reduce the heat, cover, and cook for 15 minutes, turning once.

Meanwhile, prepare a sauce by heating the lemon juice, honey, and chopped rosemary. Arrange the chicken in a serving dish and lap with the sauce. Garnish with slices of lemon and additional sprigs of rosemary (with flowers, if possible).

GARLIC ROSEMARY TUILES

Tuiles are an elegant and popular French dessert cookie, one of my favorites! They are made in the shape of a roof tile, hence their name. When flavored with rosemary and garlic, they become a tasty savory to be enjoyed as an hors d'oeuvre or snack.

2 large cloves garlic
4 tablespoons sweet butter, softened
2 tablespoons sugar
1 large egg white, at room temperature
½ teaspoon salt
4 tablespoons all-purpose flour
2 tablespoons freshly grated Parmesan cheese
about 2 tablespoons fresh rosemary leaves

Bring a small saucepan of water to the boil. Add the garlic and boil, covered, for 20 minutes. Remove the garlic and let it cool. Peel it and mash it to a paste with a fork.

Cream the butter, add the sugar, and beat the mixture until it is light and fluffy. Beat in 2 tablespoons of the garlic paste, add the egg white and the salt, and beat until the mixture is combined. Fold in the flour and the Parmesan. Transfer the mixture to a small bowl and cover it. Refrigerate for at least 4 hours or overnight.

Preheat the oven to 425 degrees F. Place rounded teaspoons of the mixture 3 inches apart on buttered baking sheets. With the back of a fork dipped in cold water, flatten the cookies carefully to make 1½-inch rounds. Sprinkle with rosemary and bake in the middle of the oven for 6 to 8 minutes, or until the edges are golden. Immediately transfer the tuiles with a spatula to a rolling pin, pressing them carefully against the pin to make them curve. Gently lift them off and set them aside to dry on a rack. The tuiles may be made up to one day in advance and kept in an airtight container.

HERB BURGERS
WITH ROSEMARY AND THYME

Part of the widespread appeal of a Florentine beefsteak is the flavor gained from delicate grilling over branches of rosemary. Try this adaptation for stove-top preparation.

½ cup onion, finely grated
3 egg yolks
½ teaspoon thyme
1 tablespoon fresh rosemary leaves, chopped
salt and freshly ground pepper to taste
2 pounds ground top round of beef
½ cup clarified butter

In a large bowl, mix together the onion, egg yolks, thyme, rosemary, salt, and pepper. Add the ground beef and blend thoroughly. Shape into rounds. In a large, heavy skillet, heat the clarified butter. Cook the burgers until seared on one side; turn and sear the other side. Serve with Cheese Bread with Six Bay Leaves (see recipe).

CHEESE BREAD WITH
SIX BAY LEAVES

The one surviving cookbook from ancient Greece and Rome is a compilation from the late fourth–early fifth century associated with Marcus Gavius Apicius, whose recipes always relied upon herbs.

1 cup dry ricotta or farmer's cheese
¾ cup unbleached flour
½ teaspoon salt
1 egg, beaten
2 tablespoons honey
6 bay leaves

Preheat the oven to 400 degrees F. Mash the cheese in a medium-size bowl until it forms a smooth, lumpless paste. Add the flour and salt; mix well with your fingers. Add the beaten egg and honey and mix all the ingredients together. The dough will be rather sticky.

Grease a baking sheet and place the bay leaves on the sheet in two star patterns. Divide the dough in half and form 2 flat loaves about ½ inch thick. Place the loaves on top of the bay leaves. Bake for 1 hour.

Cut the bread into thick slices and use for Herb Burger sandwiches. Or toast the slices and use instead of English muffins for Eggs Benedict.

SAGE POTATO CREPES

Warm potato preparations are enhanced by the strong flavor of sage. Here is a favorite.

5 large potatoes, peeled
½ cup onion, grated
1 tablespoon fresh sage leaves, chopped
8 tablespoons walnut oil
salt and freshly ground pepper to taste

Using a grater with large holes, grate the potatoes into a basin of cold water. Drain the potatoes, add the onion, and blend well. Squeeze any excess water from this mixture. Add salt, pepper, and sage, and mix all of the ingredients. Heat 1 tablespoon of oil in a non-stick 6-inch crêpe pan. When the oil is slightly smoking add ¾ cup of the potato batter. Flatten the round if it is puffy and cook about 3 minutes or until lightly browned. Turn the crêpe to the other side to brown it, and then flip it a few more times to make certain it cooks through. Repeat with the remaining batter.

Place the finished pancakes on a holding platter kept in a warm oven. Decorate with a few random sage leaves and serve hot with home-made applesauce, chilled sour cream, or Russian caviar.

BARELY COOKED TOMATO SAUCE
WITH BASIL

When you want to serve something full of flavor but you have limited time, try this delicious solution.

  2 tablespoons red wine vinegar
  salt and freshly ground pepper to taste
  about ⅓ cup fresh basil leaves, chopped
  ¼ cup plus 1 tablespoon fine olive oil
  8 very ripe Italian plum tomatoes, peeled and sliced
  1 large onion, chopped
  1 large carrot, thinly sliced
  1 tablespoon capers
  1 teaspoon garlic, minced
  1 pound tagliatelle

In a large bowl, combine the vinegar, salt, pepper, and basil. Whisk in ¼ cup oil. Add the sliced tomatoes and let marinate while you prepare the other ingredients.

In a medium saucepan, heat the butter and remaining oil over medium high heat. Add the onion and sauté until transparent. Add the carrot and capers, cook for about 1 minute, then add garlic. Stir in the tomato mixture, reduce heat to low, and cook while you prepare the pasta.

Cook the tagliatelle in a large pot of rapidly boiling salted water until the noodles are just "al dente." Drain, and immediately toss with the sauce.

AROMATIC MYRTLE BERRY VINEGAR

Myrtle berry vinegar uses the leaves, flowers, and berries from the herb. It is a pleasant way to perk up salad dressings. Or you might marinate a leg of lamb in myrtle berry vinegar for eight hours before roasting; then use the marinade to deglaze the pan.

  ½ cup of herbs
  1 pint cider or white wine vinegar

84

Make cuttings early in the day, taking a branch with leaves and berries, along with an additional tablespoon of herb leaves. Place the herbs in a wide-mouthed, heatproof jar and bruise them with a wooden spatula against the sides. In a well-ventilated kitchen, bring cider or white wine vinegar (the vinegar is more acidic) to a boil. Pour it over the leaves, filling the jar nearly to the top, and cover tightly. Let the mixture infuse for 10 days in a warm setting, shaking the jar about once a day. Taste the vinegar and if it is not strong enough, add some additional bruised leaves, but do not reboil the liquid. Strain through a sieve, discard the herbs, and filter the vinegar through some muslin or several layers of washed cheese-cloth. Bottle the vinegar in a clean wine bottle along with some fresh unbruised sprigs of myrtle, then close with a cork.

FRESH HERB BUTTERS

Herb butters can make a rather ordinary dish more inspired.

- ½ pound sweet butter
- ¼ cup herb cuttings, like parsley, dill, chives, sage, or thyme, chopped

In a large mixing bowl beat the butter until soft. Fold in the chopped herbs. Rechill the butter so that it will become firm enough to mold. Shape it into a cylinder and place it on a sheet of wax paper. Roll the butter into a 5-inch-long log and twist the edges closed. Double-wrap in tin foil and refrigerate. When ready to use, unwrap the cylinder and slice off the number of butter rounds that you'll need. Rewrap tightly and refrigerate again. If kept tightly wrapped, the butter can last for several weeks.

Try an herb butter with lemon verbena leaves; place a disk on steak. Rose geranium butter is a lightly flavored, delicious spread for cake icings and crêpe fillings. Serve it on Sunday morning muffins along with Champagne poured over fresh apricot purée.

HERBED SPICED NUTS

Herbed spiced nuts make a delicious snack or fancy treat to be placed in a dish on the table and nibbled at throughout the meal. Packed into berry boxes, they will make a most appreciated holiday gift.

    ½ cup clarified sweet butter
    2 cups salted walnuts or pecan halves, not bits
    1 tablespoon fresh rosemary, chopped
    1 tablespoon thyme leaves, no stems
    2 cups confectioner's sugar
    1 tablespoon each cinnamon, ground cloves, and nutmeg

Heat the clarified butter in a deep skillet over low heat. Add the nuts, stir, and cook over low heat for about 20 minutes, turning frequently until the nuts are lightly browned and thoroughly heated. Remove the nuts from the skillet with a slotted spoon and drain them on paper towels.

Shake the remaining ingredients together in a paper bag. Add the nuts to the bag of herb-spiced sugar and toss them until they are generously coated. Turn the nuts into a sieve and shake them to remove the excess sugar. Spread the nuts on paper towels to cool. Store herb spiced nuts in airtight containers.

HERB TOASTS

How civilized to make your own melba toasts! Nothing more than twice-baked bread, these are elegant additions to any menu and are made even more exceptional by fresh herb cuttings.

    1 loaf of an egg bread, such as a brioche or challah
    sweet butter
    fresh thyme, rosemary, oregano, dill, chives, or sage, chopped
    salt and freshly ground pepper to taste

Have the bakery cut the loaf into thin slices of ⅛ inch (or less). Preheat the oven to 400 degrees F. Melt some butter and add the herb cuttings and the salt and pepper. Brush one side of the bread slices with the butter, using a scant teaspoon per slice. Arrange the slices, buttered side up, on a baking sheet and place on the bottom rack of the oven. Bake for 5 minutes. Turn the oven off, but leave the toast in for 10 more minutes.

For breakfast toasts, flavor the butter with lavender or scented-leaf geranium; brush the toasts with bitter marmalade.

HERBED CHEESE AND SPINACH SALAD

This salad is a perfect one-course meal or an appetizer to be followed by a hearty entrée.

- ½ cup bread crumbs
- ½ cup walnuts, pulverized
- 1 tablespoon fresh thyme, dill, oregano, or tarragon leaves
- 1 8-ounce log of French goat cheese
- 2 eggs, beaten with 1 teaspoon water and salt and freshly ground pepper to taste
- 3 tablespoons walnut oil
- 1 pound spinach, washed, dried, and chilled
- vinaigrette made with sherry vinegar

Mix together the bread crumbs, walnuts, and herbs. Slice the goat cheese into 1-inch-thick rounds. Dip each round into the beaten egg mixture, then coat with the bread-crumb mixture. In a medium skillet, heat the walnut oil over medium heat. Carefully brown the cheese rounds on both sides. Remove them as they turn golden and drain on paper towels.

Toss the spinach with the vinaigrette and place on individual salad plates. Spoon a bit of the hot pan drippings over the spinach and top with a couple of cheese rounds.

WARM LEMON SPONGE SOUFFLE WITH LEMON VERBENA LEAVES

Here is a delicious dessert whose ease of preparation belies its elegance. The strong fresh flavor of lemon verbena is delicately suspended in an ethereal texture. I bake it in a double-handled copper mold, although a souffle dish is what one might expect. Present it still warm from the oven and spoon any aromatic liquid that has settled to the bottom over the servings.

> 2 whole fresh lemon verbena leaves
> 1 tablespoon butter
> ½ cup superfine sugar
> 2 tablespoons twice-sifted flour
> ½ teaspoon salt
> 3 egg yolks at room temperature, lightly beaten
> 1 cup milk
> 2 tablespoons lemon juice, freshly squeezed
> 4 egg whites, stiffly beaten
> 6 fresh lemon verbena leaves, chopped

Preheat oven to 350 degrees F. Butter the bottom and sides of a 1-quart souffle mold and place two criss-crossed lemon verbena leaves on the bottom. Mix the sugar, flour, and salt together in a large bowl. Add the beaten egg yolks and milk. Add lemon juice and chopped lemon verbena leaves. Beat egg whites until stiff and lightly fold into the mixture. Carefully and slowly, without deflating the mixture, pour it into the mold. Place the mold in pan of hot water and bake in the oven for 45 minutes. Present warm to smiling and appreciative guests.

ROSE GERANIUM JELLY

½ cup rose geranium leaves, chopped
¾ cup sugar
1 teaspoon lemon juice
¼ teaspoon vanilla
several whole rose geranium leaves

Place the chopped rose geranium leaves in a bowl and add 1½ pints of boiling water. Cover and steep for 20 minutes. Strain the liquid into a wide shallow pan, then add the sugar, lemon juice, and vanilla. Cook over medium heat until sugar is dissolved, stirring constantly so that crystals do not form on the sides of the pot. Add some fresh cut geranium leaves and let the mixture come to a rolling boil. When mixture passes jelly test (two drops flow together off a metal spoon), skim and pour into hot sterilized jars. Cover with paraffin and float a few smaller leaves on top.

LEMON VERBENA TISANE

Lemon verbena tisane is my favorite tea, herbal or otherwise. When I serve it to guests at the end of a meal it's always a soothing surprise. Tisanes are similar to teas, but fresh or dried leaves and stems—rather than fermented ones—are used to make the brew.

Pour 1 pint of just boiling water over 10 fresh lemon verbena leaves (or 1 ounce of dried leaves) in a ceramic—never metal—teapot. You can add a little honey or some dried lemon peel, but I think it's just great straight.

When you have a headcold, drink a cup of lemon verbena tisane, put some sachets filled with lemon verbena under your pillow, and look forward to a restful sleep. All herbal teas are more mellow because they lack the stimulants of caffeine and tannin; but the volatile oils are still there to give the tea its flavor.

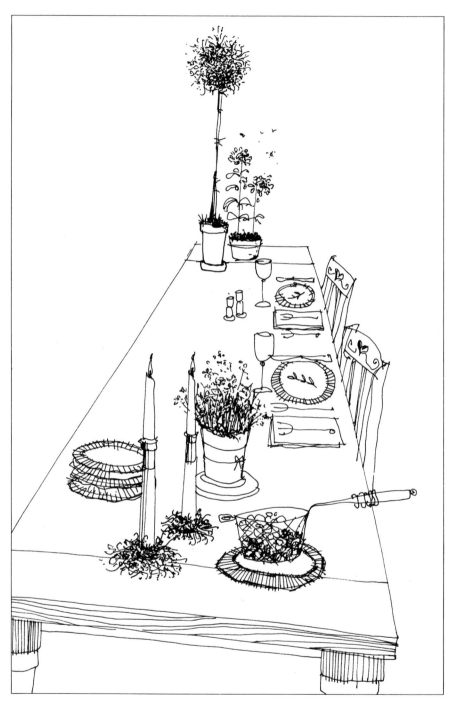

ADD HERBAL DECORATIONS AND PREPARATIONS TO EVERYDAY LIVING

USE AND DELIGHT

have tried to emphasize contemporary ideas that are based upon traditional and historical uses of herbs, as these were often both practical and charming. Most of them can be made in no time. Other than the cuttings from your own potted herbs, not much else is needed in the way of expense or dexterity.

Note: Drying herbs involves nothing more than eliminating moisture from the leaves. When harvests are as small as these, I spread my prunings on some sheets of paper and let them air-dry out of direct sunlight. To speed things up I'll place them in a warm but turned-off oven for no more than half an hour.

STREWING HERBS

In the sixteenth and seventeenth centuries long stems of freshly cut herbs were scattered over cold stone floors to take away musty odors and mask the smells of insufficient drainage.

- Start making your own sweet entrances by putting fresh stems of lavender and santolina beneath a welcome mat. As the herbs are walked over, their scent is crushed and released.
- One day some lavender prunings landed in my cat Timothy's litter box. He thought it was a nice deodorizer, much nicer than chemicals. After all, he who appreciates bushes of catnip and downy mounds of woolly thyme is entitled to strewing herbs for his own paws.
- In the fourteenth century laundresses pressed the household linen over branches of lavender, whose camphoraceous odor perfumed and prevented moth infestation. Clothes and bed linens were stored in chests filled with the sprigs of rosemary, and it was said that whoever slept on rosemary-scented sheets would be free from all evil dreams. I like to spread newly ironed items over bushy scented lavender and rosemary topiaries. They dry with a fresh garden aroma.

BOUQUETS, NOSEGAYS, AND TUSSIE-MUSSIES

Tussie-mussies were small, structured, hand-held bouquets made from strongly fragrant herbs and flowers. They were popularly carried as portable air fresheners by fashionable ladies to sniff as they daintily trod through foul streets.

In the Victorian age romantic pursuits were carried on between the high hedges of garden mazes, while clandestine flirtations were communicated through carefully composed nosegays. Even today in Italy, basil remains a lover's emblem, and, because of its powerful scent and symbolism, it continues to be featured in romantic nosegays.

Express your own thoughts with an herbal bouquet or a "poor man's nosegay." Make it from a collection of evergreen and evergrey herbs clustered around a meaningful central flower, and set it all within a paper doily.

- Tie a couple of sprigs of rosemary together with some raffia to make an herbal whisk. Send it along with a thank-you note for a recent dinner party because "Rosemary is for remembrance."
- Tuck a basting brush made by bay laurel branches into a party invitation for an outdoor barbecue. From a well-developed bay laurel plant, cut off four 6-inch-long leafy branches. Strip the leaves from the lower half of the branch. (They can be dried and saved for later use.) Wrap and tie the stems together with raffia.
- Or tie a bunch of lemon verbena branches with thin decorative ribbons and give them to your host or hostess as a "tisane-making bouquet."

WREATHS AND GARLANDS

Fashionable, beautiful, and costly, wreaths and garlands could be found in every ancient culture; the Chinese, Persians, Egyptians, and Hebrews all used them. There was a constant demand for an accessory that had five important uses: sacrificial, honorary, nuptial, sociable, and festive. It's no wonder that one-quarter of the Athenian agora, or marketplace, where peasants sold their produce, bankers had their tables, and fishmongers their stalls, was devoted to wreath sales.

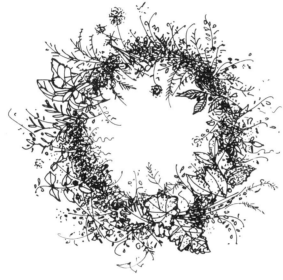

- Make a delicate herbal choker by braiding strands of embroidery floss with supple branches of sweet myrtle. Occasionally weave in some flowering stems.
- Twist together green branches of rosemary to make a pretty anklet, and wear it on the beach to keep away the sand flies.
- Or weave together several different herb branches, making the wreath large enough to encircle the brim of a straw bonnet.
- To make a traditional bridal wreath, weave together stems of rosemary, sweet marjoram, hawthorne, and orange blossoms. Add a streamer of thin satin ribbons.
- Make a miniwreath to encircle the base of fat holiday candles or to collar the necks of wine bottles decoratively while attractively catching any drips.

HOW TO START A WREATH:

- Cut supple stems from vining plants.
- Bend one whole stem to the required size. Fasten the ends together with raffia ties.
- Entwine additional stems around the first round. Allow irregular openings to occur, for these will be the spaces through which you will weave herb cuttings. Tuck in all loose ends.

Surround big, fat holiday candles with little herb wreaths, to catch the drips.

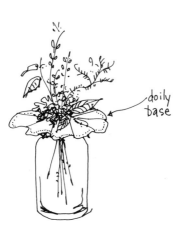

doily base

A small vase will hold a nosegay upright while you compose the herbs.

Make a small wreath as a bridal headdress. Add streamers of ribbons to match the bride's gown.

SWEET BAGS AND MOTH SACHETS

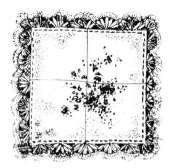

Unlike flower scents, leaf odors are quite permanent, and that is why they have always been popular for stuffings, decorations, and strewings. Herb cuttings filled cushions, bedding, and little sweet bags that were meant to keep things fresh and bug-free. Christian legend says that the baby Jesus lay on a bed of fragrant newly mowed bracken that came to be called holy clover (*Galium verum*). Sweet woodruff and lady's bedstraw are names that also aptly describe herbs that became insect-repellent stuffings when they were mixed with rushes and straw for filling mattresses. Pack up little sweet bags and moth sachets of dried lavender, rosemary, pennyroyal, santolina, sweet marjoram, crushed cloves, and lemon peel. Put some of the mixture in the center of 5-inch squares of fabric. Gather up the corners like a hobo's sack, bunch the neck together, and tie it closed with a ribbon.

- Hang them in closets, from the arms of chairs, or tucked in sweater drawers.
- Use as "toe sachets" and stuff your shoes in a refreshing way.
- And don't forget "mouse sachets" for your favorite feline. Gather bundles of dried catnip in furry velour pouches, with long bow ties for the tails.
- Give a bride sweet bags of sweet marjoram for her trousseau.

ENTERTAINING IDEAS

Throughout history hosts and hostesses have relied upon impressive effects to entertain and surprise their guests. Louis XIV outdid them all at Versailles, where hidden jets of water showered the unsuspecting as they meandered around his pleasure gardens. On a more gracious level, crystallized confections delighted the Jacobeans and were described by Sir Hugh Platt in *Floraes Paradise* (1608). It included instructions for making "flowers candied as they grow . . . so that you may bid your friends after dinner to a growing banquet."

Little Trees with Candied Leaves

Using myrtle and lavender topiaries, brush some leaves on both sides with egg white. Dust lightly with powdered sugar, "while holding a paper under to receive the sugar that falleth by and in three hours it will candie or harden upon."

Silvered Herbs for Special Occasions

Still intact and buried in tombs of the fourth and fifth century B.C. are examples of delicate and exquisite silver bridal wreaths of myrtle, woven with berries and flowers. For the ultimate garnish, embellish branches of herb foliage with real silver. Thin and delicate foil sheets of edible silver, known as *vark*, are available at Indian specialty stores.

Frozen Herbal Decanters

For an unusual holiday preparation, perhaps to serve with celebratory caviar, set a bottle of akvavit or vodka in an empty milk carton. Pour preboiled water into the carton. Tuck in herbal greenery and freeze. The liquor will become syrupy but not solid. When the herbal water has frozen, peel off the carton. Borrow a stopper from a fancy crystal decanter to top it off.

Herbal Ice Cubes

Fill an ice-cube tray just short of the rim, using freshly boiled water that has come to room temperature (to make it clear). Add some pretty herb sprigs and blossoms or whole leaves of scented geraniums. Freeze; serve with sangria, iced tea, or lemonade.

PREPARATIONS FROM A STILLROOM

To some people stillrooms conjure up the haunts of Macbeth's witches, where muslin bags bob on seething waters in iron cauldrons. There is no contemporary counterpart to the seventeenth-century stillroom. At best it might be considered a combination home laboratory, pantry, medicine cabinet, and storeroom. The setting came to symbolize the domestic life of that period, the place where the lady of the manor cultivated proper

Store dried herbs in small individual portions for incense

Store herb seeds in little glassine envelopes that stamp collectors use

Stuff little sweet bags with dried herbs

Fill little bottles with herb-scented inks

Pour herb refresheners into assorted bottles

Catnip sachets for the 'mouser'

housewifely arts. It was here that she directed her maids in the preparation of herbal concoctions, personal toiletries, and distillations meant for her household and members of her parish poor.

These are some contemporary applications you can prepare after you've collected your herbal cuttings in the stillness of your own rooms.

Herbal Handbath

To make a real treat for gardeners' working hands, use an herb infusion of either thyme, lavender, lemon verbena, rosemary, pennyroyal, or myrtle leaves. Fill one-quarter of a wide-mouth jar with herbs that have been crushed against the sides of a bowl with a wooden spoon. Pour unscented alcohol from the neighborhood drugstore to within an inch of the top. Cover tightly and set this aside for two weeks in a shady location, occasionally shaking up the bottle. Pour 2 tablespoons of liquid soap into the mixture and repack into your own little cough-medicine bottles, secured with a stopper.

Fragrant Rubbing Lotion

For a pleasant facial refresher with lovely natural scents, make an herbal infusion using witch hazel with sprigs of fresh lavender or lemon verbena. Add a handful of herb leaves to a half-pint of liquid. Seal the jar and let the ingredients steep for two weeks in a warm spot. Strain the liquid and repack it into a clean bottle, while floating an herb sprig in it for identification. Close with a stopper.

Herbal Brow Wraps

Roll several small washcloths tightly around stems of lemon verbena, santolina, lavender, or rosemary. Tie the ends closed with some raffia. Steam them in the top of a double boiler. Let them dry and later wrap them individually. When the herbal compress is resteamed and set over the forehead and eyes, its fragrant warmth will pleasantly soothe an aching head. Give them as stocking stuffers to worried friends with furrowed brows.

Herbal Incense

After drying leaves of lemon verbena, rosemary, santolina, and lavender, rub each herb separately through a fine sieve, then store in small individual bottles. When necessary, put a handful in a Pyrex dish or votive candle holder and light a little mound of fragrance to dispel tobacco, fish, and other unpleasant odors.

Herb-Scented Ink

Make a strong decoction of highly scented herbs like lemon verbena, rosemary, or lavender. Slowly boil the leaves for an hour in order to extract the aromatic essences that are water-soluble. Add 1 teaspoon of this liquid to a bottle of ink.

Packets of Herb Seeds

Dry some seeds from one of your favorite herb plants, or collect exotic ones on your next vacation. Remember that herbs from warm climates make indoor plants in the North. Pack them into tiny glassine envelopes—the kind that stamp collectors use. Label with the date of collection and the herb variety. You might want to include a photo or a small sketch of the mature herb plant.

And finally, to make the prettiest gift-wraps, tie all of your little presents with ribbon or thin green florist's string and sprigs of fresh herbs.

EPILOGUE

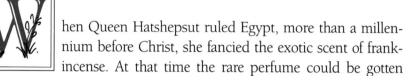

hen Queen Hatshepsut ruled Egypt, more than a millennium before Christ, she fancied the exotic scent of frankincense. At that time the rare perfume could be gotten only from the gum of the Boswellia tree, native to the land of Punt (Somalia). In due course a mission was sent to East Africa and specimens of the tree were collected and brought back to Egypt's dry and windy land. They were individually transplanted into earthenware vessels and carefully placed within walled oases that became the first enclosed courtyards in gardening history. We will never really know whether this was to display the rare and foreign greenery or to give it conscientious attention, but the plantings flourished.

Uprooting trees, shrubs, flowers, and herbs from their native habitats and transporting them to alien settings has always been a common form of amusement and one-upmanship in gardening. Louis XIV had armies of men move tubbed citrus trees into the orangeries at Versailles for half the year, while Victorian conservatories were packed right up to their glass roofs with status symbols of towering potted palms and tropical ferns. Even today regal scale is attempted by corporations that compete to containerize the biggest ficus trees for their headquarters' lobbies. In a world where elements of nature have become powerful playthings and external reminders of someone's ability to command and impose his or her way, seemingly humble potted herbs take on even more significance as objects of gentle delight.

Potted herbs form tranquil settings while emphasizing the virtues of simple beauty. In an area that might be impossible to underplant, grow what is possible with that which is portable. Plant a potted herbal path on a crushed gravel footway where nothing else might take. Foster a fragrant promenade along a common property line with decorative pots of herbs. Or create whimsical green architecture on tar roofs while camouflaging unsightly views with a landscape of herbal topiaries. Use obelisks, pyramids, and spheres of potted herbs if your garden longs for the strong architectural elements of grand stairs, fountains, and statues of bygone eras. Add interest to the center of a vegetable garden and mark the time of day by surrounding a sundial with a variety of potted herbs.

Make a temporary location homey and hospitable in a hurry by landscaping the entry with a potted herb garden. And when it's time to leave, move your garden with you. Perhaps the herbal topiaries grown at your first summer rental will become the crowning glory of your ultimate manse.

Bring nature into the confines of your home, while adding gardens of beguiling greenery to otherwise lifeless locations. Even in winter the aroma of herbs will re-create images of sunshine and summertime. Pots of herbs have subdued hues that will lend a quiet elegance to rooms and table settings, without taking on any grand airs. Construct interior green architecture with herbal topiaries when architectural detail is lacking. Give a nondescript flight of stairs some character by punctuating the treads with a line-up of herbal standards. Use spirited and fragrant potted herbs to enliven tabletop still-lifes. As a lovely welcome in an entry hall, arrange a fragrant forest of scented herbs and get rid of those dusty bowls of potpourri. Put these enchanting forms of living decoration anywhere that a vase of flowers might go. Skip the floral centerpiece and landscape a dinner table with an arbor of tiny herb trees, remembering that an "arbor" was an "herber" in Old English.

But best of all, turn a garden-watcher into a gardener. Share your pleasure and give a potted herb as a long-lasting gift to a friend who longs for a garden, even on the smallest scale. It will yield all of the same hopes, frustrations, and ultimate satisfactions for those who do their cultivating in a pot of terra cotta, rather than a plot of terra firma. Virgil said it best: "Admire a large estate, but work a small one."

BIBLIOGRAPHY

Books don't happen without other books. From the many old, new, and treasured volumes that I used, I would like to mention a partial list for inspiration and information.

Ancient Roman Gardens. Colloquium on the History of Landscape Architecture. Edited by Elisabeth MacDougal, and Wihelmina Jashemski, Dumbarton Oaks, Washington, D.C., 1981.

Bailey, Liberty Hyde and Ethel Zoe, *Hortus Third: A Concise Dictionary of Plants Cultivated in the United States and Canada.* Macmillan, New York, 1978.

Beck, Thomasina, *Embroidered Gardens.* Viking, New York, 1979.

Blomfield, Reginald, *The Formal Garden in England.* 1892. Reprint. Waterstone & Co., London, 1985.

Blunt, Wilfred, *The Art of Botanical Illustration.* Collins, London, 1950.

Clarkson, Rosetta E., *Herbs: Their Culture and Use.* Collier, Macmillan, London, 1942.

Curtis, Charles H. and Gibson, W., *The Book of Topiary.* 1904. Reprint. Charles E. Tuttle Co., Rutland, Vermont, 1986.

D'Andrea, Jeanne, *Ancient Herbs.* J. Paul Getty Museum, Malibu, California, 1982.

Esplan, Ceres, *Herbal Teas, Tisanes and Lotions.* Thorsons Publishers Ltd., Wellingborough, Northamptonshire, 1981.

Garden Lore of Ancient Athens. American School of Classical Studies of Athens, Princeton, New Jersey, 1963.

Gilbertie, Sal, *Herb Gardening at Its Best.* Atheneum, New York, 1978.

Godfrey, Walter H., *Gardens in the Making.* B. T. Batsford, London, 1914.

Gordon, Lesley, *A Country Herbal.* Webb & Bower, Exeter, 1980.

Graf, Alfred Byrd, *Exotic Plant Manual.* Roehrs Co., East Rutherford, New Jersey, 1970.

Hadfield, Miles, *Topiary and Ornamental Hedges.* Adam & Charles Black, London, 1971.

Herbs for Use and for Delight. An Anthology from The Herbalist. Published by the Herb Society of America. Reprint. Dover Publications, New York, 1974.

Huxley, Anthony, *Huxley's Encyclopedia of Gardening*. Universe Books, New York, 1982.

Jekyll, Gertrude, *Garden Ornament*. 1918. Reprint. Antique Collectors Club, Ltd., Woodbridge, Suffolk, 1982.

Langley, Batty, *New Principles of Gardening*. London, 1728.
Lawson, William, *The Country House-wife's Garden*. 1617. Reprint. Breslich and Foss, London, Third Ed., 1983.
Lloyd, Nathaniel, *Garden Craftsmanship in Yew and Box*. Ernest Benn, Ltd., London, 1925.

Moldenke, Harold N. and Alma L., *Plants of the Bible*. 1952. Reprint. Dover Publications, New York, 1986.

Northcote, Lady Rosalind, *The Book of Herbs*. John Lane, London, 1921.

Oxford Companion to Classical Literature, The. Compiled by Sir Paul Harvey, Oxford University Press, New York, 1986.

Peplow, Elizabeth and Reginald, *Herbs and Herb Gardens of Britain*. Webb & Bower, Exeter, 1984.
Propagation for the Home Gardener, Vol. 40, No. 1. Brooklyn Botanic Garden Record, 1984.

Rodale Herb Book, The. How to Use, Grow and Buy Nature's Miracle Plants. Edited by William H. Hylton, Rodale Press, Emmaus, Pennsylvania, 1983.
Rohde, Eleanour Sinclair, *A Garden of Herbs*. Philip Lee Warner, London, 1932.
————, *Herbs and Herb Gardening*. The Medici Society, London, 1936.

Trained and Sculptured Plants, Vol. 17, No. 2. Brooklyn Botanic Garden Record, 1982.
Tuan, Yi-Fu, *Dominance and Affection, The Making of Pets*. Yale University Press, New Haven, 1984.

THE END*

*And the beginning, *"For the love of gardening is a seed that once sown never dies, but always grows and grows to an enduring and ever increasing source of happiness."*

Gertrude Jekyll

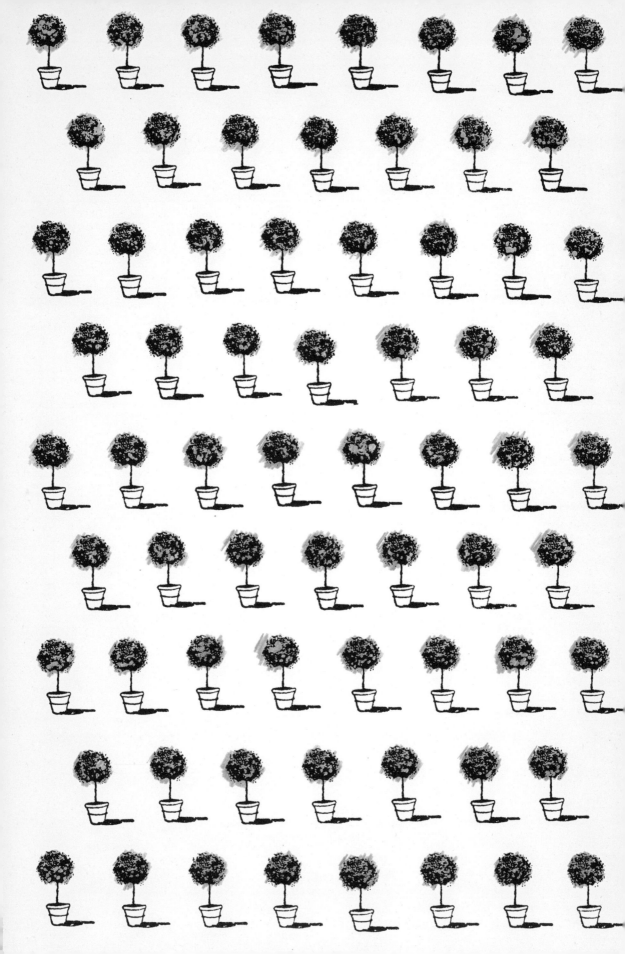